EXPLORERS
AND
EXPLORATION

POLO, MARCO – SHACKLETON, ERNEST HENRY

Marshall Cavendish
New York • London • Singapore

Marshall Cavendish
99 White Plains Road
Tarrytown, New York 10591-9001

www.marshallcavendish.com

Consultants: Ralph Ehrenberg, former chief, Geography and Map Division, Library of Congress, Washington, DC; Conrad Heidenreich, former historical geography professor, York University, Toronto; Shane Winser, information officer, Royal Geographical Society, London

Contributing authors: Dale Anderson, Kay Barnham, Peter Chrisp, Richard Dargie, Paul Dowswell, Elizabeth Gogerly, Steven Maddocks, John Malam, Stewart Ross, Shane Winser

MARSHALL CAVENDISH
Editor: Thomas McCarthy
Editorial Director: Paul Bernabeo
Production Manager: Michael Esposito

WHITE-THOMSON PUBLISHING
Editors: Alex Woolf, Steven Maddocks, and Alison Cooper
Design: Ross George and Derek Lee
Cartographer: Peter Bull Design
Picture Research: Glass Onion Pictures
Indexer: Fiona Barr

ISBN 0-7614-7535-4 (set)
ISBN 0-7614-7543-5 (vol. 8)

Printed in China

08 07 06 05 04 5 4 3 2 1

Library of Congress Cataloging-in-Publication Data

Explorers and exploration.
    p. cm.
  Includes bibliographical references (p.) and index.
  ISBN 0-7614-7535-4 (set : alk. paper) -- ISBN 0-7614-7536-2 (v. 1) -- ISBN 0-7614-7537-0 (v. 2) -- ISBN 0-7614-7538-9 (v. 3) -- ISBN 0-7614-7539-7 (v. 4) -- ISBN 0-7614-7540-0 (v. 5) -- ISBN 0-7614-7541-9 (v. 6) -- ISBN 0-7614-7542-7 (v. 7) -- ISBN 0-7614-7543-5 (v. 8) -- ISBN 0-7614-7544-3 (v. 9) -- ISBN 0-7614-7545-1 (v. 10) -- ISBN 0-7614-7546-X (v. 11)
  1. Explorers--Encyclopedias. 2. Discoveries in geography--Encyclopedias. I. Marshall Cavendish Corporation. II. Title.
  G80.E95 2005
  910'.92'2--dc22

2004048292

ILLUSTRATION CREDITS

AKG London: 647 (Andrea Jemolo), 649, 650, 653, 662, 665, 673, 675 (Keith Collie), 681, 703.

Art Archive: 663 (Doges' Palace, Venice / Dagli Orti).

Bridgeman Art Library: 651 (Index), 654, 655, 659, 660, 661, 666, 668, 669 and 672 (New York Historical Society), 671, 674 (Smithsonian Institution, Washington, DC), 682, 683 (Index), 685, 688, 704, 705 (Index), 706, 707 (Royal Geographical Society), 712 (The Stapleton Collection).

NASA: 644, 645, 646, 676, 677, 679, 680, 691, 692, 693, 694, 696, 697, 698, 701.

Peter Newark's American Pictures: 664.

Royal Geographical Society, London: 648, 652, 656, 657, 658, 686, 709, 710, 711, 713, 715.

Science Photo Library: 678 (U.S. Geological Survey), 689, 690 (NOVOSTI), 695 (NASA), 699 (NASA), 700 (NOVOSTI), 702 (NASA).

Topham Picturepoint: 716, 718.

Cover: David Livingstone's sextant (Bridgeman Art Library).

color key	time period
▬▬▬	to 500
▬▬▬	500–1400
▬▬▬	1400–1850
▬▬▬	1850–1945
▬▬▬	1945–2000
▬▬▬	general articles

CONTENTS

POLO, MARCO   **564**

PONCE DE LEÓN, JUAN   **569**

PORTUGAL   **573**

POWELL, JOHN WESLEY   **577**

PROVISIONING   **581**

PRZHEVALSKY, NIKOLAY   **585**

PTOLEMY   **589**

QUIRÓS, PEDRO FERNÁNDEZ DE   **594**

RALEIGH, WALTER   **598**

RECORD KEEPING   **601**

REMOTE SENSING   **605**

RICCI, MATTEO   **608**

RUSSIA   **612**

SACAGAWEA   **616**

SATELLITES   **619**

SCANDINAVIA   **624**

SCOTT, ROBERT FALCON   **628**

SETI (SEARCH FOR EXTRATERRESTRIAL INTELLIGENCE)   **632**

SHACKLETON, ERNEST HENRY   **635**

Glossary   **639**

Index   **640**

POLO, MARCO

MARCO POLO WAS BORN in 1254 in the city-state of Venice, in northern Italy, and died there in 1324. He and his family were the first Europeans since ancient times to reach China by traveling overland across central Asia. Marco Polo's famous book about his travels, *Il Milione*, provided a fascinating insight into the life and geography of an area of the world that was little known to fourteenth-century Europeans. Long after Marco Polo's death, *Il Milione* was a source of inspiration to numerous European explorers.

Below **This sixteenth-century fresco, from a villa in western Italy, portrays Marco Polo in old age.**

LURE OF THE EAST

Marco Polo was born into a family of noble Venetian merchants. In the thirteenth century Venice was becoming a prosperous center for trade between Asia and Europe, and in 1260 Marco Polo's father and uncle, Niccolò and Maffeo, set off on a trading mission to Bukhara (in present-day Uzbekistan) and China (known at the time as Cathay). In 1266 Niccolò and Maffeo were welcomed into the court of Kublai Khan (c. 1216–1294), the khan (emperor) of the Mongols. Kublai Khan had become head of the Mongol Empire in 1259 and in the same year proclaimed himself emperor of China and established his capital at Beijing.

Niccolò and Maffeo were as intrigued by the flamboyant Kublai Khan as he was by their culture and background. Deeply impressed by their stories about Europe, the emperor commissioned the Polo brothers to return home and carry messages from him to the pope. He requested that they come back to Beijing with a hundred educated men to teach him about Christianity.

By the time the brothers arrived back in Venice in 1269, Marco had reached the age of fifteen, and his mother had died. Pope Clement IV had died the previous year, in 1268, but a successor had not yet been appointed. Indeed, it was not until 1271, when

ASSIA

Gregory X was invested as pope, that the Polo brothers were supplied with letters and precious gifts to take to China. When the Polos set off on their second trip to China, at the end of 1271, they were accompanied by two friars, who were instructed to teach Kublai Khan about Christianity. They were also joined by young Marco.

LONG JOURNEY

The Polos took four years to reach Beijing. Having left Venice by ship, they traveled via Jerusalem to Ayas (present-day Yumurtalik, in southeastern Turkey), where they witnessed fighting between the Armenians and the Egyptians. Afraid to travel any farther, the friars turned back, but the Polos continued their journey through Persia toward central Asia.

Above **This illustration, which shows Marco Polo and his uncles crossing the deserts of Asia by camel caravan, is taken from a fourteenth-century atlas drawn in Catalonia (a region of northeastern Spain).**

The Silk Road

Chains of Muslim traders transported spices, jewels, and silk to Europe from places as far away as northern China along an ancient overland trade route known as the Silk Road. The four-thousand-mile (6,400 km) Silk Road passed through the Gobi Desert, Samarkand (in present-day Uzbekistan), and Antioch (in present-day Turkey) to ports in Greece, Italy, the Middle East, and Egypt. For centuries European traders considered the long journey through Muslim-controlled territory too dangerous to use themselves. In the thirteenth and fourteenth centuries, the Mongols made the ancient highway safer, and increasing numbers of European merchants and holy men began to make the journey east.

At Badakhshan (in Afghanistan) Marco fell ill, and the travelers were forced to rest. Setting off again a year later, they passed over the mountains of the Hindu Kush and the Pamirs (known as the roof of the world). The next leg of the journey took them through the vast and desolate Gobi Desert, described years later in Marco's account of his travels as being "so long that it would take a year to go from end to end. . . . It consists entirely of mountains and sands and valleys. There is nothing at all to eat."

AT THE COURT OF KUBLAI KHAN

The Polos arrived at Shang-tu, the summer palace of Kublai Khan, in May 1275. They

1254
Marco Polo is born in Venice, Italy.

1260
Niccolò and Maffeo Polo begin their first journey to China.

1266
Arrive at the court of Kublai Khan in Beijing.

1269
Return to Venice.

1271
Marco Polo accompanies his father and uncle on a journey to China.

1275
Arrives in China and is welcomed to the summer palace of Shang-tu by Kublai Khan.

1275–1292
Is appointed by Kublai Khan to a number of administrative posts and travels throughout China.

1292
Kublai Khan grants permission for Marco, Niccolò, and Maffeo to return to Venice.

1295
The Polos arrive back in Venice.

1298
Imprisoned during the war between Genoa and Venice, Marco begins recounting his adventures to a fellow prisoner.

1324
Dies in Venice.

A description of the Yangtze River at Yiyang:

In the amount of shipping it carries and the total volume of traffic it exceeds all the rivers of the Christians put together and their seas into the bargain. I give you my word that I have seen in this city fully five thousand ships at once, all afloat in this river . . . I assure you that the river flows through more than sixteen provinces, and there are on its banks more than two hundred cities, all having more ships than this . . . fully two hundred thousand craft pass upstream every year and a like number return.

Marco Polo, *Il Milione*

found that the royal courts of Europe were no match for the luxury and splendor of the Mongol court. Marco admired the powerful and charismatic ruler and averred that he had never in his life seen anything so beautiful as the khan's palace. The English Romantic poet Samuel Taylor Coleridge (1772–1834) immortalized this palace as Xanadu in his 1816 poem "Kubla Khan."

In November 1275 the Polos left Shang-tu to take up residence at the winter palace in Beijing. Marco was astounded by the magnificent buildings of the capital and impressed by the customs and way of life of the people. By now Marco and Kublai had become good friends, and the khan employed the young Venetian in an administrative role. In the following years Marco was sent on many official missions, including trips to Yunnan (a province in southern China), Burma, Cochin China (present-day Laos and southern Vietnam), and southern India. For three years Marco also acted as the khan's personal representative in the city of Yang-chou, a short distance north of the Yangtze River.

Below **For their journeys to and from China, Marco Polo and his family followed a course that connected land and sea routes used by traders since ancient times.**

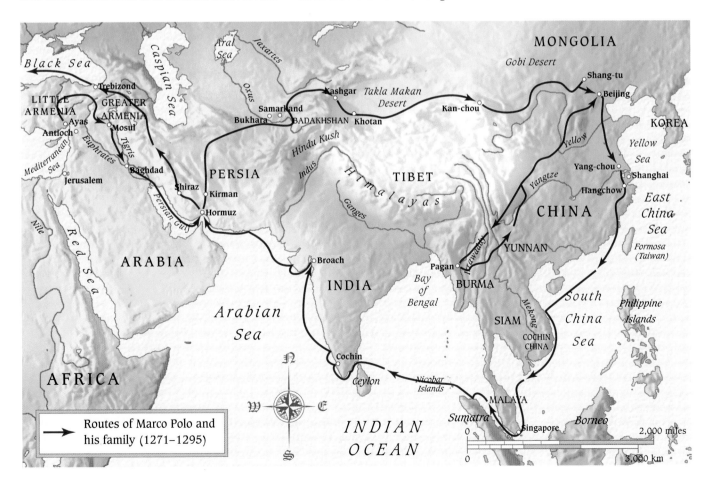

Routes of Marco Polo and his family (1271–1295)

A Traveler's Tales

As the khan grew old, the Polos began to fear that a future ruler would not treat them so well. After they had spent seventeen years in his court, the elderly khan reluctantly allowed them to return home, and they reached Venice in the winter of 1295. By 1298 Marco was commanding a galley in a war between Genoa and Venice. When the Venetians were defeated, Marco was thrown into jail for one year. He was placed in a cell with a writer named Rusticello of Pisa. To pass the time, Marco recounted his adventures in the East, and Rusticello wrote them down.

Il Milione, also known as *The Book of Ser Marco Polo the Venetian Concerning the Kingdoms and Marvels of the East*, was published after Marco Polo's release from jail and became a best-seller. Many readers found the stories difficult to believe, but years later Marco claimed, "I did not write half of what I saw." Marco was contented to spend the rest of his life with his family in Venice, where he died in 1324. His book provided source material for some of the first accurate European maps of Asia and inspired numerous later explorers, including Christopher Columbus, who in 1492 set out on a voyage to reach Cathay by sailing west.

Chinese Society

Marco Polo was impressed by the orderly way in which a highly organized network of officials ran a country as vast as China. Although many dialects were spoken throughout the country, by using a single system of writing, officials were able to communicate with each other. China developed a postal system using first- and second-class services, and its civilization was the first to use paper money.

Above **This fourteenth-century French illustration depicts Kublai Khan bidding farewell to Niccolò and Marco Polo. The Italians are given an imperial letter of safe conduct, a sort of passport that guarantees their safety as long as they remain in Mongol territory.**

SEE ALSO
• Caravan • Silk Road

PONCE DE LEÓN, JUAN

THE SPANISH CONQUISTADOR AND EXPLORER Juan Ponce de León (1460–1521) was a key figure in Spain's early conquest of territories in the New World (the Americas). Ponce de León established the first European settlement on Puerto Rico and governed the colony there from 1509 to 1512. In 1513 he became the first European to explore Florida. During the Florida voyage, Ponce de León and his pilot, Anton de Alaminos, discovered the existence of the Gulf Stream, a tidal current whose use dramatically shortened the journey across the Atlantic for Spanish ships returning home.

Below **Juan Ponce de León, the Aragonese explorer of Florida.**

LOYAL SOLDIER

Born into noble Spanish society, as a boy Juan Ponce de León served as a page to King Ferdinand at the court of the Kingdom of Aragon. While in his late teens he joined the army that, in 1492, drove the Muslim Moors out of the southern province of Granada and thereby reclaimed Granada for the Spanish crown. The following year Ponce de León joined Christopher Columbus's second voyage across the Atlantic (1493–1496). During the voyage, Columbus added the sightings of Dominica and the lesser Antilles to his investigations of the major Caribbean islands of Cuba and Hispaniola, where he landed on his first voyage.

Ponce de León evidently believed that his future lay in the New World, for in 1502 he returned to the Caribbean. He served as a military commander in the large force led by Nicolás de Ovando (c. 1451–c. 1511), the recently appointed governor of Spain's New World territories. On the island of Hispaniola, the native Taino people were in revolt against the Spanish settlers, and Ponce de León played an important part in the Europeans' suppression of the islanders' rebellion. Ovando rewarded Ponce de León by appointing him governor of an area of eastern Hispaniola.

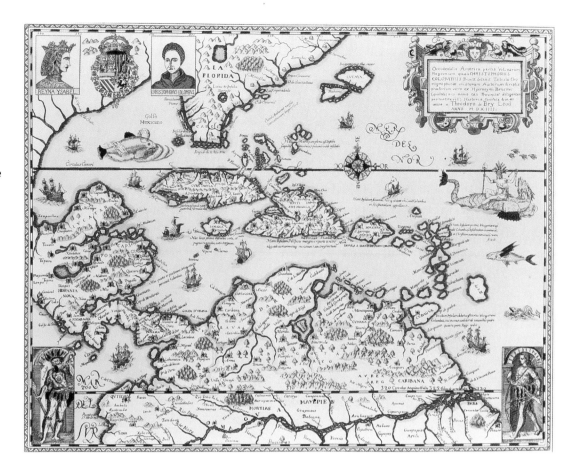

Right **Produced in the late sixteenth century by the Flemish engraver Theodore de Bry, this map was among the first to show the Caribbean Sea, its islands, and the surrounding mainland with reasonable accuracy.**

PUERTO RICO

While he was on Hispaniola, Ponce de León heard reports from the Taino that the neighboring island of Borinquen was rich in gold. Enchanted by the lure of this supposed treasure island, in 1508 he set out for Borinquen and soon afterward claimed it for the Spanish crown. In 1509 he was appointed the first governor of the island, renamed Puerto Rico (Spanish for "rich port"), and established a settlement at Caparra (near present-day San Juan).

FLORIDA

In March 1513 Ponce de León set out on a new expedition, in search of an island known as Bimini, which was thought to lie somewhere to the north of Cuba. On Bimini, it was reported, there flowed a spring or fountain whose waters cured all diseases and gave the drinker eternal youth. Three ships headed northwest, and around Easter, Ponce de León sighted a land that he named Florida. The name derives from the Spanish name for the Easter festival, *Pascua Florida*, and perhaps also

1460
Juan Ponce de León is born at San Servas, Campos, Spain.

1490–1492
Takes part in the fight to expel the Moors from Granada.

1493
Sails on Christopher Columbus's second voyage to the Americas.

1502–1504
Serves in a force commanded by Nicolás de Ovando that restores Spanish control over Hispaniola.

1503
Becomes governor of part of Hispaniola.

1508–1509
Conquers and explores Puerto Rico.

1509–1512
Serves as governor of Puerto Rico.

1513
Discovers Florida.

1514
Is made governor of Florida.

1521
Is fatally wounded during an attempt to establish a settlement in Florida.

from the region's florid (lush and flowery) vegetation.

Ponce de León landed somewhere south of the present-day city of Saint Augustine on April 2, 1513, and claimed Florida (which he still thought of as an island) for Spain. From Saint Augustine the expedition sailed down the east coast as far as the Florida Keys, before heading north along the west coast. The hostility of Florida's native people prevented the Spaniards from exploring inland. Instead, they returned to Puerto Rico via Cuba.

Ponce de León returned to Florida in 1521 with a commission from King Ferdinand to colonize the territory. The expedition landed near Estero Bay on the Gulf of Mexico, on Florida's western coast. The site was not well chosen, as it lacked both fresh water and accessible food supplies. In desperation Ponce de León led a force inland to seek provisions. A group of native people ambushed the men, and in the fight Ponce de León was badly wounded in the leg by a reed arrow.

The Fountain of Youth

*T*he existence of a fountain that bestows immortality on anyone drinking its waters recurs in several ancient legends. In one ancient Greek myth the nymph Arethusa is turned into a fountain located on a mysterious island somewhere in the Mediterranean. Several sixteenth-century explorers imagined that this island (which they named Bimini) might in fact be located in the New World. Ponce de León's fruitless search for Bimini is memorialized in Fountain of Youth Park in Saint Augustine, Florida.

This military setback left the already weary and starving settlers further weakened by injury and sickness. They had little choice but to abandon their enterprise and return to Cuba. There, in July 1521, Ponce de León died from his wounds.

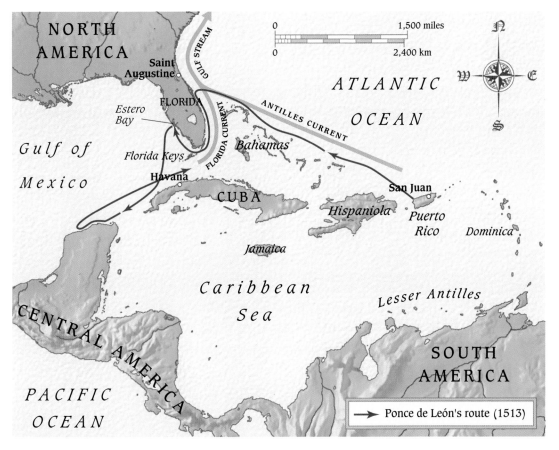

Left **Although he failed to locate the fabled island of Bimini or to penetrate into Florida, Ponce de León's accidental discovery of the Gulf Stream was an important milestone in the Spanish conquest of the Americas.**

0   1,500 miles
0   2,400 km

NORTH AMERICA

Saint Augustine

GULF STREAM

FLORIDA

Estero Bay

Florida Keys

FLORIDA CURRENT

ANTILLES CURRENT

ATLANTIC OCEAN

Gulf of Mexico

Havana

Bahamas

CUBA

San Juan

Hispaniola

Puerto Rico

Dominica

Jamaica

Caribbean Sea

Lesser Antilles

CENTRAL AMERICA

SOUTH AMERICA

PACIFIC OCEAN

→ Ponce de León's route (1513)

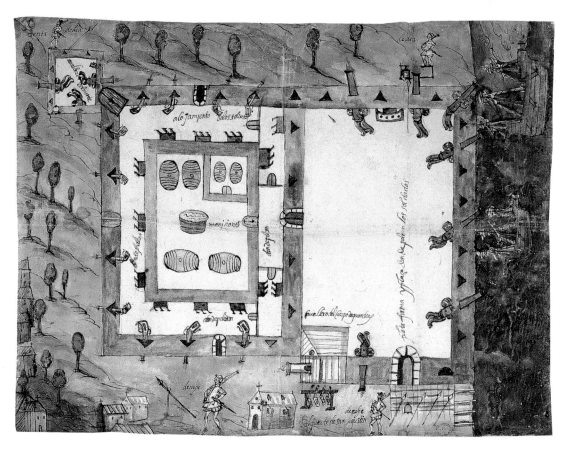

Right **Founded by Pedro Menéndez de Avilés in 1565 on a site visited by Ponce de León in 1513, Saint Augustine, Florida, is the oldest continuously settled European city in North America. This bird's-eye view of the earliest Spanish fort there dates from 1577.**

Christopher Columbus describes the Taino people of Hispaniola:

All whom I saw were young, not above thirty years of age, well made, with fine shapes and faces; their hair short, and coarse like that of a horse's tail, combed toward the forehead, except a small portion which they suffer to hang down behind, and never cut. . . . Weapons they have none, nor are acquainted with them, for I showed them swords which they grasped by the blades, and cut themselves through ignorance. They have no iron. . . . They are all of a good size and stature, and handsomely formed.

Christopher Columbus,
Journal of the First Journey

DISCOVERY OF THE GULF STREAM

During their voyage around the tip of Florida in April 1513, Ponce de León and his navigator Antonio de Alaminos had noticed a powerful current sweeping northwest. Later, by sailing with this current rather than across it, as earlier navigators had done, they found that it was part of a system of currents that rotate clockwise around the North Atlantic and thus offered Spanish ships a speedier and safer route back to Europe than the more southerly route they had been using.

SUCCESS AND FAILURE

The conquest and settlement of the New World during the early sixteenth century was a remarkable undertaking. The achievements of Ponce de León, in common with those of other Spanish conquistadores, depended on a personality that blended determination and courage with ruthlessness toward any native peoples who were considered hostile and aggressive. Although Ponce de León failed to find a fountain of eternal youth, he gained immortality of a sort by achieving the settlement of Puerto Rico and the discovery of Florida and the Gulf Stream.

SEE ALSO

- Columbus, Christopher • Ferdinand and Isabella
- Narváez, Pánfilo de • Spain

PORTUGAL

IN THE FIFTEENTH CENTURY Portugal became the first European power to send ships out on long voyages of exploration. Early Portuguese voyages were motivated by the desire to find new trade routes as well as by ambition to send Christian soldiers into a holy war against Islam. Portuguese ships sailed west into the Atlantic and south along the coast of Africa, from where, after rounding the Cape of Good Hope, they crossed to India, the East Indies (present-day Indonesia), and China. In the sixteenth century the Portuguese created a great empire whose power depended, not on the conquest of vast areas of land, but on the seizure of key ports, which were used to control maritime trade routes.

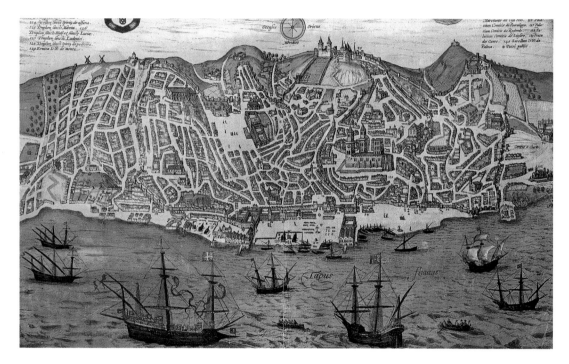

Left **This map of the Portuguese capital of Lisbon, which dates from the sixteenth century, includes images of some of the ships that helped create the Portuguese Empire.**

HOLY WAR

Portugal's overseas expansion began in 1415, when King John I (reigned 1385–1433) sent a fleet to North Africa to fight against the Muslims who ruled there. John and the nobles who fought for him saw themselves as crusaders fighting a holy war on behalf of Christianity. They succeeded in capturing the key Muslim port of Ceuta.

John's son, Prince Henry (1394–1460), played a leading part in the capture of the North African territory. Henry, later called Henry the Navigator because of his important role in encouraging Portuguese voyages of exploration, realized that Ceuta was a rich trading center. Camel caravans had been bringing gold dust north across the Sahara Desert, but the trade had stopped as soon as Ceuta was in the hands of the Portuguese. Henry wanted to find the source of the gold, which lay somewhere in the African interior, and decided that the only way to avoid traveling through the Muslim-held lands of North Africa was to sail down the coast.

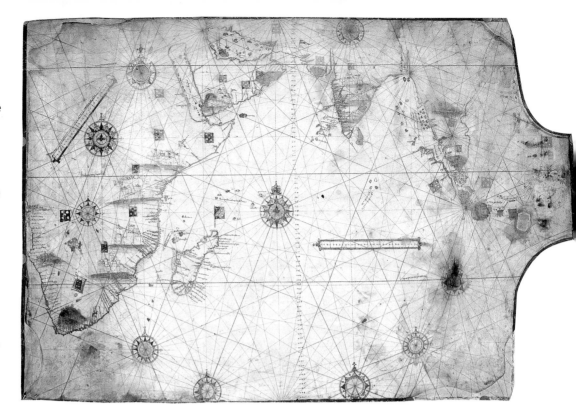

Right **The success of the Portuguese Empire was helped greatly by the ability of Portuguese cartographers to make accurate maps of newly discovered regions. This 1518 sea chart is centered on the Indian Ocean and includes Madagascar, India, Burma, Thailand, the Malay Peninsula, and Sumatra.**

EXPLORATION OF THE AFRICAN COAST

In 1419 Henry set up his court at Sagres, on Portugal's southern coast. He brought together mapmakers, navigators, and shipbuilders and used their expertise to organize a program of exploration of the African coast. His navigators mapped the coast as far as present-day Sierra Leone and traveled up the Senegal and Gambia Rivers.

Exploration of the west coast of Africa was given further impetus in the 1470s, when King Afonso V (reigned 1438–1481) awarded a five-year trade monopoly to Fernão Gomes. According to the deal, Gomes was allowed exclusive rights to trade any goods he found on condition that he explore one hundred leagues (about 370 miles, or 600 km) of new coastline each year. Gomes discovered that, south of Guinea, the African coast turned sharply to the east. This discovery raised Portuguese hopes that they had reached the southernmost point of Africa (whose extent was unknown at that time) and that they would soon find a direct sea route to India—the source of spices that could be sold in Europe for a huge profit. Portuguese hopes were dashed when the coast was found to turn to the south once again.

1415
John I seizes the North African port of Ceuta from the Muslims.

1419
Henry the Navigator begins his program of geographical exploration.

1469–1475
Fernão Gomes's ships explore two thousand miles (3,200 km) of Africa's western coast.

1482–1485
Diogo Cão explores as far south as Namibia (southwestern Africa).

1488
Bartolomeu Dias rounds the southern tip of Africa.

MAY 21, 1498
Vasco da Gama reaches India.

1500
Pedro Álvares Cabral sails to India by way of Brazil and in doing so establishes Portugal's right to territorial claims in South America.

1509
Francisco de Almeida seizes Indian ports on the Malabar coast from Muslim traders.

1511
Afonso de Albuquerque's conquest of Malacca gives Portugal control of the sea route to the Moluccas (Spice Islands).

1517
The Portuguese reach Canton, China.

1519–1522
Ferdinand Magellan, a Portuguese navigator in the employ of the Spanish, captains the first fleet to sail around the world.

1602
The Dutch East India Company is founded.

1641
Dutch forces seize Malacca.

The following words open a Portuguese poem written in 1572 in praise of the founders of the Portuguese Empire and particularly of the voyage made by Vasco da Gama to India:

This is the story of heroes who, leaving their native Portugal behind them, opened a way to Ceylon, and further, across seas no man had sailed before. They were men of no ordinary stature, equally at home in war and in dangers of every kind: they founded a new kingdom among distant peoples, and made it great.

Luís Vaz de Camões, *The Lusiads* (1572)

THE ROUTE TO INDIA

In the 1480s a new king, John II (reigned 1481–1495), sent Diogo Cão on two voyages of exploration in search of a route to India. Although he explored a further 1,500 miles (2,400 km) of coast for the Portuguese, Cão could not find Africa's southern tip. The continent was much larger than anyone had suspected.

It was Bartolomeu Dias, also sponsored by John II, who located and rounded Africa's southern tip in 1488. The tip was named the Cape of Good Hope, because the way to India and its riches now lay open. The route across the Indian Ocean was pioneered by Vasco da Gama, who reached India in May 1498.

Below **In this sixteenth-century Flemish tapestry the most famous of all Portuguese explorers, Vasco da Gama, is shown reaching Calicut, India, in May 1498.**

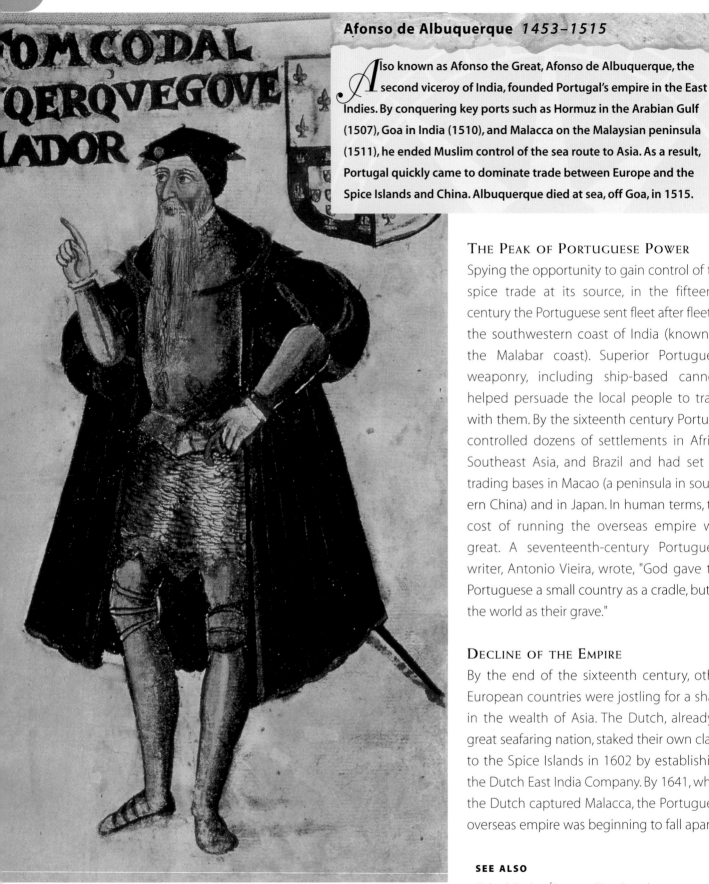

Afonso de Albuquerque 1453–1515

Also known as Afonso the Great, Afonso de Albuquerque, the second viceroy of India, founded Portugal's empire in the East Indies. By conquering key ports such as Hormuz in the Arabian Gulf (1507), Goa in India (1510), and Malacca on the Malaysian peninsula (1511), he ended Muslim control of the sea route to Asia. As a result, Portugal quickly came to dominate trade between Europe and the Spice Islands and China. Albuquerque died at sea, off Goa, in 1515.

Above **A sixteenth-century painting of Afonso de Albuquerque in full armor, his finger raised in a gesture of command.**

THE PEAK OF PORTUGUESE POWER

Spying the opportunity to gain control of the spice trade at its source, in the fifteenth century the Portuguese sent fleet after fleet to the southwestern coast of India (known as the Malabar coast). Superior Portuguese weaponry, including ship-based cannon, helped persuade the local people to trade with them. By the sixteenth century Portugal controlled dozens of settlements in Africa, Southeast Asia, and Brazil and had set up trading bases in Macao (a peninsula in southern China) and in Japan. In human terms, the cost of running the overseas empire was great. A seventeenth-century Portuguese writer, Antonio Vieira, wrote, "God gave the Portuguese a small country as a cradle, but all the world as their grave."

DECLINE OF THE EMPIRE

By the end of the sixteenth century, other European countries were jostling for a share in the wealth of Asia. The Dutch, already a great seafaring nation, staked their own claim to the Spice Islands in 1602 by establishing the Dutch East India Company. By 1641, when the Dutch captured Malacca, the Portuguese overseas empire was beginning to fall apart.

SEE ALSO

- Cabral, Pedro Álvares • Dias, Bartolomeu
- Gama, Vasco da • Henry the Navigator
- Magellan, Ferdinand • Netherlands

POWELL, JOHN WESLEY

JOHN WESLEY POWELL (1834–1902) GAINED FAME for his heroic boat journey down the Colorado River—unexplored until that time—and through the Grand ·Canyon. He developed a deep attachment to the American West and spent the rest of his life promoting scientific exploration, the preservation of Native American culture, and the judicious use of the natural resources of the West.

Below **While serving as an artillery captain in the Union army during the American Civil War, Powell lost his right arm.**

CHILDHOOD AND EDUCATION

John Wesley Powell's mother and father moved from Britain to the United States in 1830. His father preached in Methodist churches, and the family moved many times. As a result, young Powell's education was often interrupted. He left home at age sixteen and settled in Illinois, where he taught himself enough to get a job as a teacher. In the late 1850s he made several trips along the Mississippi and other rivers and became well known in Illinois as a scientist.

WAR SERVICE

In 1861 the American Civil War broke out between the northern and southern states. Although there were a number of disagreements between the two sides, the principal point of conflict was the issue of slavery, which the South claimed the right to practice. Fiercely opposed to slavery, Powell enlisted to fight for the North. In a battle in 1862, he suffered a wound that forced doctors to amputate his right arm at the elbow. Nevertheless, he returned to combat and served until January 1865, a few months before the North won the war.

SEEDS OF EXPLORATION

After the war, Powell returned to Illinois to teach college. In the summers of 1867 and 1868, he led expeditions that explored parts of the Rocky Mountains region. On the second trip, he saw some of the canyons cut by the Colorado River. His interest aroused, in 1869 he launched his biggest expedition to date—a boat trip down the Colorado.

This excerpt from Powell's diary of the 1869 trip captures the feelings of excitement and anxiety felt by many explorers:

We are ready to start on our way down the Great Unknown. . . . We are three quarters of a mile in the depths of the earth, and the great river shrinks into insignificance as it dashes its angry waves against the walls and cliffs that rise to the world above. . . . We have an unknown distance yet to run; an unknown river yet to explore. What falls there are, we know not; what rocks beset the channel, we know not; what walls rise over the river, we know not. Ah well! We may conjecture many things. The men talk as cheerfully as ever; jests are bandied about freely this morning; but to me the cheer is somber and the jests are ghastly.

John Wesley Powell,
The Exploration of the Colorado River and Its Canyons

Right **Powell and his men needed more than three months for the grueling journey down the Green and Colorado Rivers. "Every waking hour passed in the Grand Canyon," he wrote, "has been one of toil."**

DOWN THE COLORADO

Powell and nine others launched their four boats on the Green River in southwestern Wyoming on May 24, 1869. It was a daring journey, the first of its kind down a river that has dangerous rapids. Just two weeks into the trip, one of the boats was destroyed when it smashed into a huge boulder. The dangers were especially great for the one-armed Powell, who at times had to be tied into his seat on the boat because, with only one hand, he could not hold on securely. On one occasion he fell and clung to a cliff until another member of the party rescued him.

By July 17 the party had reached the point where the Green River enters the Colorado. In mid-August the men prepared to enter the Grand Canyon. The rapids there were so pow-erful that the explorers had to row their boats in single file in order to pass through. They grew short of food, and on August 28 three of the group decided to leave. (After climbing to the canyon rim, they were killed by a band of Native Americans.) The remaining explorers pushed on down the river. On August 29 they finally emerged from the canyon after travel-ing nearly nine hundred miles (1,450 km). "The relief from danger and the joy of success are great," Powell wrote. The American public hailed him and his men as heroes.

THE SECOND EXPEDITION

Two years later, Powell led another expedition down the Colorado River. In the years between, he taught himself geology and eth-nology, the study of native cultures. On the

1834
John Wesley Powell is born in New York.

1852
Begins teaching.

1855–1858
Carries out personal explorations of the Mississippi River.

1861–1865
Serves in Union army in Civil War; loses right arm.

1865
Becomes a professor at Illinois Wesleyan College.

1867–1868
Leads two expeditions to the West.

1869
Explores the Colorado River.

1871
Leads second Colorado expedition.

1879
Becomes director of Bureau of Ethnology.

1881
Becomes director of U.S. Geological Survey.

1902
Dies at summer home in Maine.

1871 trip his team mapped much of the Colorado basin and studied the agricultural potential of that dry region. Powell sent a group, led by Almon Thompson and Frederick Dellenbaugh, to explore farther north. The team explored and named the previously unknown Escalante River and the Henry Mountains.

Above **This U.S. Geological Survey map of the Yellowstone Park region is drawn with the precision typical of the maps created under Powell's direction.**

BUREAUCRAT AND SCIENTIST

Powell continued to organize scientific studies in the West, some of which he led himself. His work won support and, more important still, vital funding from the U.S. Congress. Eventually he left teaching to take up posts in the new government agencies that were being formed to oversee the study of the West. On the staff of the U.S. Geological Survey from 1875, he succeeded Clarence King as director in 1881.

As director of the U.S Geological Survey, Powell inaugurated the publication of official bulletins, monographs, and charts. In one of the many reports he helped to produce, Powell introduced new geological theories to explain how the Grand Canyon had been formed. He wrote about the need to preserve Native American culture. He also promoted the careful use of resources in the West. His work caused conflict with some political and business leaders, who feared he would block the profitable use of those resources. Eventually, political pressure forced Powell to leave the Geological Survey in 1894. He kept his other job—head of the Bureau of American Ethnology—until his death in 1902.

SEE ALSO

• Mapmaking • Native Peoples
• Natural Resources • Surveys

PROVISIONING

BEFORE THE SIXTEENTH CENTURY, sea travel generally involved sailing short distances along a charted coast. Ships called in at ports along the route to take on fresh provisions (supplies of food and drink). In the Age of Discovery, explorers seeking direct ocean routes to East Asia spent many days far from the sight of land—and for this reason far from accessible supplies of fresh food and water. On such transoceanic voyages the lack of fresh food presented a serious problem. Illness and disease were common and in many cases fatal. Provisioning is similarly troublesome in desert and polar regions; later explorers of such regions found it extremely difficult to maintain a healthy diet.

Left **This 1911 photograph shows members of the ill-fated Antarctic expedition of Robert Scott (far right) eating in their tent. The sledging rations of tea, cocoa, butter, sugar, biscuits, and powdered meat provided far less energy than the six thousand calories the men burned every day.**

DRINKING SUPPLIES

All explorers have to plan their journey so as to ensure that they reach supplies of freshwater regularly. In icy climates, as long as it is possible to start a fire, explorers can drink water from melted ice or snow. In deserts or at sea, however, finding freshwater is more problematic.

By the sixteenth century, it was common knowledge that alcoholic drinks, such as beer and wine, remain drinkable for a long time. Consequently, liquor rather than water was the main drink on European ships. From 1500, Spanish and Portuguese ships carried a wine allowance of about two-and-a-half pints (1.5 liters) per man per day. English ships carried one gallon (4.5 l) of beer per man per day, though from the early nineteenth century, a rum ration of ten fluid ounces (approximately 0.25 l) began to replace beer. Ships setting out on ocean crossings or long tours of duty carried rations to last six months. Beer barrels took up approximately one-third of the hold on an English ship.

Alcohol, with its high carbohydrate content, provided between twenty and twenty-five per cent of the crew's energy requirements. However, a major drawback of the reliance on liquor was drunkenness, which frequently caused fights and accidents—such as crew members falling from the ship's rigging. Another drawback was the tendency of alcohol to worsen the effect on the body of poor nutrition.

Water was carried on board ships in wooden barrels that, before being filled, were cleaned by burning them on the inside. Water was used mainly for soaking salted foods, rather than for drinking. Foods such as salted pork and cod, for example, had to be soaked for twenty-four hours in frequent changes of water before they could be eaten.

FOOD SUPPLIES

Before the invention of canning and refrigeration, ships carried a mixture of fresh and preserved foods. In hot climates fresh food lasted no more than a week, so sailors were grateful for any fish they could catch. In all but the largest vessels, food was cooked on a fire lit in an iron firebox situated amidships. Sailors used charcoal to light the fire and then burned coal. Because of the risk of flames spreading to the wooden ship itself, fires were lit only in calm conditions.

Foods were preserved by drying, salting, or pickling in brine. The simplest dried food was hardtack. Made from flour and water and baked ashore, it was cheap and easy to store. As long as it was kept dry and was not attacked by weevils (insect pests), hardtack

Right **This can of roast veal, which was prepared in 1823 for William Parry's voyage to the Canadian Arctic, was opened some 116 years later, in 1939. Its contents, found intact, had not been touched.**

The explorer John Ross reports on the hardships his 1829 Arctic expedition suffered owing to the lack of provisions:

. . . being forced by want of provisions and the approach of a most severe winter [we returned] to Fury Beach. . . . Our sufferings, aggravated by want of bedding, clothing, and animal food, need not be dwelt upon . . . [but] we were reduced to the last stage of debility. . . . We left Fury Beach on July 8, carrying with us three sick men which were unable to walk, and in six days we reached the boats, where the sick daily recovered.

From a letter to the secretary to the Board of Admiralty, 1833

Left **Like so many other Arctic explorers, the Scotsman John Ross (1777–1856) experienced the effects of inadequate provisioning.**

could last for months. Among the other dried foods that appeared regularly in a ship's inventory were peas, beans, and cheese. Salt pork was regular sailors' fare.

The standard daily food ration per person on English ships was approximately one pound of hardtack or bread every day, one pound of salt beef or salt pork with peas on Sundays, Mondays, Tuesdays, and Thursdays, and four ounces of salt fish (ling or cod) on Wednesdays, Fridays, and Saturdays. The fish was commonly supplemented with cheese, butter, or olive oil. This diet lasted for at least 250 years in the English navy; the rations supplied on other European ships were very similar. Together with the alcohol ration, a sailor's diet provided approximately 4,500 calories per day. Although this diet met the sailors' energy needs for the work they had to do, the rations contained no vitamin C and virtually no vitamin A. The health problems resulting from these deficiencies became worse during longer journeys or while wintering in cold climates.

James Lind *1716–1794*

Born and educated in Edinburgh, James Lind joined the Royal Navy as a surgeon's assistant in 1739. In 1747 he carried out an experiment to discover the best treatment for scurvy. Lind selected six pairs of scurvy sufferers from his ship, HMS *Salisbury,* and gave each pair different additions to their usual diet. One pair was given a quart of cider each day, one was given seawater, and another had to eat a mixture of garlic, horseradish, and mustard. Two pairs were given medicine. The final pair was given two oranges and one lemon every day. This last pair made a dramatic recovery.

In 1754 Lind published his results in *A Treatise of the Scurvy.* Although he had demonstrated that citrus fruits were better than any other remedy for scurvy, it was forty years before naval ships were ordered to carry supplies of lemon juice.

Above **Through careful experimentation, the Scottish surgeon James Lind demonstrated that citrus fruits help to prevent scurvy.**

Poor Nutrition

Until the twentieth century there was scant knowledge of what constituted a healthy, balanced diet, of the way the nutritional needs of the body change in relation to the demands placed upon it, and, most important for explorers, of the energy value of particular foods. Among the dietary diseases common before the eighteenth century was scurvy. Sailors spending long periods without eating fresh food frequently suffered scurvy, a disease caused by a lack of vitamin C (ascorbic acid), a nutrient found in fresh fruit and vegetables. Scurvy is marked by aching joints and dry skin and hair, as well as by exhaustion and bleeding gums and body organs. Severe cases of scurvy led to death. As early as the seventeenth century, some naval captains understood that scurvy could be prevented fairly simply by a regular intake of fresh citrus fruits or fruit juices, foods rich in vitamin C. Regular rations of lemon juice did not become the norm, however, until the mid-eighteenth century.

SEE ALSO

• Illness and Disease

Przhevalsky, Nikolay

A RUSSIAN ARMY OFFICER WITH AN INTEREST IN GEOGRAPHY, Nikolay Przhevalsky (1839–1888) was sent by the Russian imperial authorities to explore the vast, uncharted region of central Asia. Przhevalsky was the most successful of many adventurers who traveled to central Asia. He made four major journeys into Mongolia, China, Turkistan, and Tibet between 1870 and 1885, and the books he wrote describing his experiences opened up the region to western European as well as to Russian eyes.

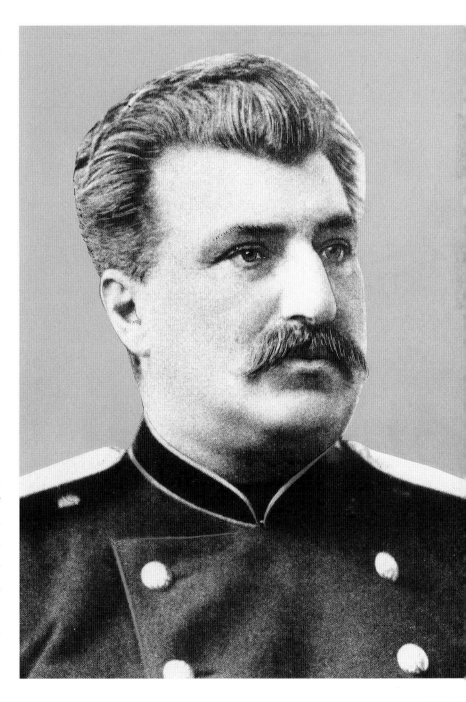

Below **By the time of his death in 1888, Przhevalsky was a Russian hero, as is suggested by his pose in this undated photograph.**

The Great Game

Nikolay Przhevalsky entered the Russian army as a junior officer and gained promotion quickly. From 1864 to 1866, he taught geography at the Warsaw Military Academy, before volunteering for a posting to Irkutsk in Siberia in 1867. He spent his first three years there carrying out a census of the people and writing about the geography and natural history of the Ussuri River region.

In the nineteenth century central Asia was bounded by the Russian Empire to the north and by the British Empire on the Indian subcontinent to the south. Both empires hoped to win power and influence in the region (their rivalry was known as "the great game.") The first move of both powers was to send out explorers and agents to produce maps and records of central Asia.

Expeditions in Central Asia

Between 1870 and 1873 Przhevalsky was engaged in his first major exploration of central Asia. With two companions, he crossed the Gobi Desert and traveled over the A-la Shan, a desert plateau on the frontier between Tibet and Mongolia. Summer temperatures on the A-la Shan reach 98°F (37°C), but winter temperatures can fall as low as −26°F (−32°C). Przhevalsky frequently suffered from bouts of terrible thirst.

Right **This map shows Przhevalsky's pioneering routes through central Asia on his third and fourth journeys.**

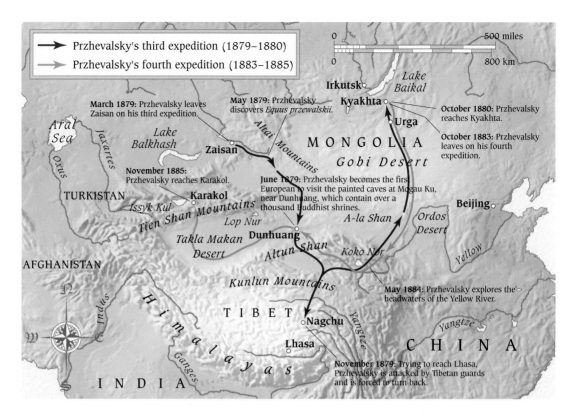

Przhevalsky's third expedition (1879–1880)
Przhevalsky's fourth expedition (1883–1885)

March 1879: Przhevalsky leaves Zaisan on his third expedition.

May 1879: Przhevalsky discovers *Equus przewalskii*.

October 1880: Przhevalsky reaches Kyakhta.

October 1883: Przhevalsky leaves on his fourth expedition.

November 1885: Przhevalsky reaches Karakol.

June 1879: Przhevalsky becomes the first European to visit the painted caves at Mogau Ku, near Dunhuang, which contain over a thousand Buddhist shrines.

May 1884: Przhevalsky explores the headwaters of the Yellow River.

November 1879: Trying to reach Lhasa, Przhevalsky is attacked by Tibetan guards and is forced to turn back.

The 1870–1873 expedition was vast in its scope. Przhevalsky visited Urga (the present-day Mongolian capital of Ulan Bator) before crossing the Gobi Desert to Beijing. He explored the upper reaches of the Hwang Ho, or Yellow River, and then crossed China from east to west using an ancient caravan route that took him to Lake Koko Nor (Tsing Hai). His published description of this journey, translated into English as *Mongolia, the Tangut Country and the Solitudes of Northern Tibet*, was a best-seller. Przhevalsky received honors and medals from geographical societies all over the world as a result of his expedition.

On his second expedition, in 1876 and 1877, Przhevalsky reached the lakes of Lop Nur in northwestern China and discovered the Altun Shan range that borders Tibet on the north. He was almost certainly the first European to catch sight of Lop Nur since the visit to the region of the Venetian traveler Marco Polo in the late thirteenth century. Returning to Tibet in 1879, Przhevalsky spent a year traveling widely through its northern and central regions. On his fourth journey, between 1883 and 1885, he ranged across the high mountains that separate Mongolia from Tibet.

1839
Nikolay Przhevalsky is born near Smolensk in western Russia.

1855
Is commissioned as an officer in the Russian army.

1867
Is posted to the Ussuri region near Irkutsk, in Siberia, where he begins a study of the local geography and people.

1870–1873
On his first expedition, crosses the Gobi and Ordos Deserts and reaches Lake Koko Nor.

1876–1877
On his second expedition, crosses the Tien Shan range and the Takla Makan Desert; reaches Lop Nur; discovers the Altun Shan range and attempts to reach Lhasa.

1879–1880
Explores northern and central Tibet on his third expedition; gets to within 125 miles (202 km) of Lhasa.

1883–1885
Explores the headwaters of the Yellow River; continues westward to Issyk-Kul, a lake.

1888
Dies at Karakol, in Turkistan.

Przhevalsky's Horse

*I*n the early nineteenth century, scientists believed that the wild horse was extinct. Naturalists were excited when, in 1877, Przhevalsky reported rumors of herds of wild horses in the high plains near the Altai Mountains. As proof, Przhevalsky exhibited a skull and a hide given to him by local border guards. On his third journey into central Asia, near the edge of the Gobi Desert, he observed two herds of the wild horse that now bears his name.

Przhevalsky's horse (*Equus przewalskii*) resembles a large pony. The animals were able to survive for long periods without water on the cold, windy plains at heights of over eight thousand feet (2,400 m), where pasture is limited. The last wild herd was spotted in the Gobi Desert in 1968; over two hundred of these remarkable animals survive in zoos and reservations around the world.

On all four of his expeditions, Przhevalsky studied the plants and animals that he found on his travels. Like many other nineteenth-century explorers, he was also a collector. He gathered over 20,000 zoological and 16,000 botanical specimens. His most famous discoveries are a species of wild camel and the wild horse that was named after him.

Below **Przhevalsky's horse is a hardy animal with short legs, a short neck, and a stiff standing mane. Przhevalsky noted that the animals also have excellent hearing, good eyesight, and a sharp sense of smell.**

The Forbidden City

*F*rom the point of view of many nineteenth-century Europeans, the mountainous land of Tibet was one of the most mysterious places in the world. Its capital, Lhasa, was sealed off from the rest of the world by the Himalayas to the south and by the vast Tibetan plateau to the north. Although Lhasa was an important destination for Buddhist pilgrims, Europeans were not allowed to approach the city—which for this reason became known as the Forbidden City.

Tibet was ruled by the Dalai Lama, the supreme head of the Dge-lugs-pa (Yellow Hat) order of lamas (Buddhist spiritual leaders). When a Dalai Lama died, his soul was believed to pass into the body of an infant born forty-nine days later. That infant would be taken to the Palace of Potala and installed as the next ruler of Tibet.

Above Built in 1645 on the site of a seventh-century shrine, the Potala Palace, once the home of the Dalai Lama, was Tibet's holiest place.

QUEST FOR THE FORBIDDEN CITY

Przhevalsky tried several times to reach Lhasa, Tibet's capital. In 1873 he was forced to turn back when supplies ran short just twenty-seven days' journey from Lhasa. In 1879 he was attacked by Tibetan guards who feared that he was planning to capture the Dalai Lama, the supreme Buddhist spiritual leader.

In September 1888 Przhevalsky set out once more from Irkutsk. On this, his fifth expedition, he hoped that he would finally reach Lhasa. By the beginning of November, he had reached the shores of Issyk-Kul (a lake in present-day Kyrgyzstan). While exploring the extent of the lake, Przhevalsky contracted typhoid, probably after drinking from an infected stream, and died. The place of his death, Karakol, was renamed Przhevalsk in his honor.

SEE ALSO
- Caravan • Polo, Marco • Russia • Silk Road
- Younghusband, Francis Edward

PTOLEMY

THE WORK OF CLAUDIUS PTOLEMY (C. 85–170 CE), perhaps the greatest geographer, mathematician, and astronomer of the ancient world, represents a culmination of the scientific achievements of his age. His astronomical books offered a way of looking at the universe that remained the standard view for almost 1,500 years after his death, and his geographical work greatly influenced European explorers at the beginning of the Age of Discovery.

MYSTERIOUS LIFE

Little is known about the life of Claudius Ptolemy. He is known to have spent his working life in the city of Alexandria in Egypt, the center of Greek and Roman learning in the ancient world. There can be little doubt that he used Alexandria's famous library, which contained an estimated 500,000 hand-written scrolls.

Ptolemy's name may be a clue to his ethnic and political origins. His nomen, or family name, Claudius, suggests that an ancestor of his had been granted the honor of Roman citizenship, perhaps by Emperor Claudius (reigned 41–54 CE). His cognomen, or personal name, Ptolemy, indicates that he was descended from Macedonian Greeks, who came to Egypt as part of the army of Alexander the Great (356–323 BCE). In short, Ptolemy was a culturally complex figure (one of a great many in the ancient Mediterranean world): an Egyptian who spoke Greek and Latin and had the status of a Roman citizen.

PTOLEMY THE ASTRONOMER

Ptolemy's most important surviving work is the *Almagest*, a monumental study of astronomy that he compiled in thirteen books. The *Almagest* (a title that means "the greatest compilation") is essentially a textbook. It describes in great detail the movement and positions of celestial bodies—the sun, the moon, and the five known planets. It is also a catalog of the stars as seen from Alexandria.

Below **This wooden statue of Ptolemy, carved around 1470, forms part of the choir stalls in a church in Ulm, southwestern Germany.**

Ptolemy's achievement was to bring together in a single broad study the sum of all Greek astronomical knowledge. He did so by gathering together the great variety of work of earlier astronomers—such as Hipparchus, to whom he makes reference. The *Almagest* is a scholarly synthesis in which Ptolemy put Greek knowledge of astronomy into order.

Ptolemy also added many observations of his own, including his conception of a geocentric (earth-centered) universe. He argued that Earth was at the center of the solar system and that the planets and the Sun orbited it. Mercury, the closest celestial body to Earth, was followed by Venus, the Sun, Mars, Jupiter, and finally Saturn. This view of the universe, soon widely accepted, became known as the Ptolemaic system.

Ptolemy's *Almagest*, with its clear text and logical arrangement, soon became the standard work on astronomy, while the work of other astronomers, including Hipparchus, faded into obscurity. The *Almagest* stood the test of time and was used for fourteen centuries, first by Arabic astronomers and later by European astronomers. Only in the early six-

Below **This engraving, dating from the 1660s, depicts the Ptolemaic view of the universe, with Earth at its center and the celestial bodies orbiting in concentric circles around it.**

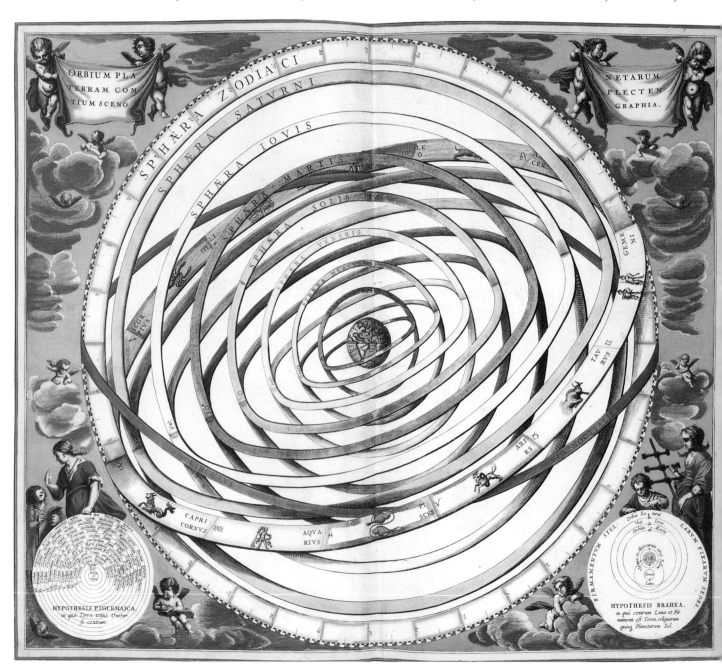

teenth century, when the Polish astronomer Nicolaus Copernicus (1473–1543) formulated his theory of a heliocentric (sun-centered) solar system, was the Ptolemaic system superseded.

PTOLEMY THE GEOGRAPHER

Ptolemy's geographical work also stood the test of time and was of enormous value to geographers throughout the Middle Ages. His eight-volume *Guide to Geography* was an attempt to map the entire world as it was known in the second century. Although none of the maps drawn by Ptolemy himself survive, numerous print editions and manuscripts were produced in the centuries following his death, and his maps were still being used by cartographers and explorers in the fifteenth century.

Six of the books in the *Guide to Geography* constitute a list of eight thousand places

Above **This fourteenth-century relief of Ptolemy observing the heavens is one of a series found at the Campanile (bell tower) in Florence, Italy.**

(both settlements and topographical features), with their latitude and longitude. The system of coordinates had been in use for about four hundred years at the time Ptolemy applied it to his own work. He acknowledges that his list was partly based on the work of an earlier scholar, Marinus of Tyre, about whom nothing more is known. However, Ptolemy was the first geographer to make extensive use of geographical coordinates to pinpoint the location of features on a map.

Classical Learning, Lost and Found

After the collapse of the Western Roman Empire in the fifth century CE, there was a general decline in scholarly and artistic activity in Europe (the period until 1000 is sometimes known, in whole or in part, as the Dark Ages). However, many works of ancient Greek and Roman scholarship, including Ptolemy's *Almagest* and *Guide to Geography*, were preserved in the libraries of the Arab world, where they were copied and translated into Arabic (the title *Almagest* derives from its Arabic name, *Al-Majisti*).

Ptolemy's works and many others remained lost to western Europe until the early fifteenth century, when Arabic scholars started to bring the classical texts to Constantinople. They were translated into Greek, taken to western Europe, and translated into Latin, the language used by European scholars. The rediscovery of texts that had been lost for a thousand years led to a period known in Europe as the Renaissance (literally, "rebirth"), because it was marked by a reawakening of interest in the classical period.

One of Ptolemy's most important contributions to the science of mapmaking was his work on map projection. In common with other scholars of his day, Ptolemy recognized that the earth was a sphere and gave advice on how best to represent its curved surface on a flat chart. He also gave instructions for drawing a world map and issued twenty-six detailed maps of particular areas.

Ptolemy lived long before the invention of printing. The production of books involved laborious copying, by hand, from one manuscript to another. It was all too easy for mistakes to creep in, and Ptolemy, whose maps depended on absolute mathematical accuracy, was clearly anxious to prevent copyists from introducing errors into his work. He gave a list of instructions for the map copyists to follow, which helped them to redraw his maps as accurately as possible—and enabled cartographers many hundreds of years later to reconstruct Ptolemy's maps without sight of the originals.

To draw his famous world map, Ptolemy used a variety of sources. It was possible in only a few cases to arrive at an accurate calculation of a place's latitude, and accurate methods of calculating longitude had not been devised. So Ptolemy had to rely heavily on travelers' itineraries, particularly the reports of merchants and of the Roman armies. These itineraries gave lists of settlements, waymarkers, and posting stations and the relative distances between them. It was from this information that Ptolemy constructed his view of the world, and, unsurprisingly, his map is accurate in the area of the Roman Empire and adjacent regions but vague and inaccurate for areas outside the Roman sphere of influence.

Ptolemy's biggest miscalculation, which was due largely to the impossibility of measuring longitude accurately, was to underestimate the circumference of the earth

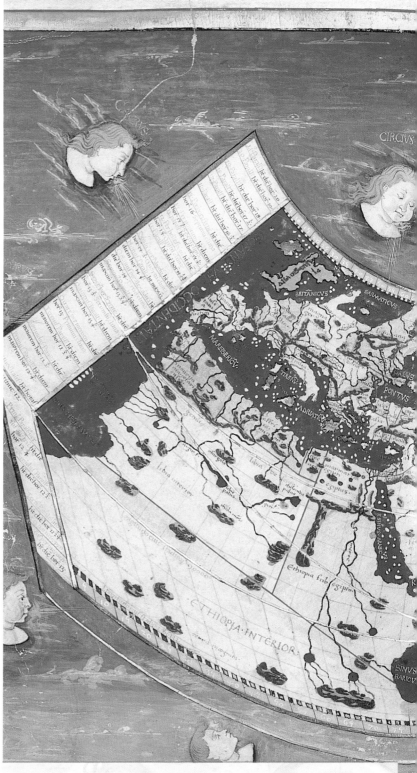

c. 85 CE
Ptolemy is born in Egypt.

c. 127–141
Makes astronomical observations from Alexandria, Egypt.

c. 146–170
Studies in Alexandria and produces many works, the greatest of which are the *Almagest* and *Guide to Geography*.

c. 170
Dies in Alexandria.

In the introduction to his great geographical work, Ptolemy defines the science of geography:

Geography is the graphic representation of the known world as a whole. . . . It differs from chorography in that chorography takes single regions separately and deals with them individually, embracing every smallest detail, such as creeks, hamlets, villages, the reaches of rivers and such things; while the function of geography is to display the known world as a coherent unity, dealing with the nature and location only of such things as are suitable to a general and universal description, such as gulfs, great cities and nations, the more notable rivers and similar outstanding things in each category.

Ptolemy, *Guide to Geography*, book 1

by 40 percent. This misinformation led Christopher Columbus, in the fifteenth century, to believe that Asia lay merely a short distance away across the Atlantic, within easy reach of Europe. Another pervasive misconception was Ptolemy's belief that the Indian Ocean was a landlocked sea, bounded to the south by a great southern continent (known as *Terra Australis*). Not until Bartolomeu Dias rounded the Cape of Good Hope, at Africa's southern tip, in 1488 was this theory disproved. Explorers continued to search for the southern continent into the eighteenth century.

Above **The world known to and mapped by Ptolemy encompassed Europe, Asia, and part of Africa. This medieval reconstruction of Ptolemy's famous world map also includes graphical representations of the twelve winds.**

SEE ALSO

- Astronomy • Geography • Hipparchus
- Latitude and Longitude • Mapmaking
- Map Projection • Southern Continent

Quirós, Pedro Fernández de

THE PORTUGUESE NAVIGATOR Pedro Fernández de Quirós (1565–1615) sailed on two Spanish voyages of exploration west from South America across the Pacific. In 1492 Christopher Columbus had taken Christianity from Europe to the New World (the newly discovered territories in the Americas), and Quirós envisaged himself as a second Columbus, chosen by God to take Christianity to another new world. The territory Quirós hoped to explore, conquer, and Christianize was *Terra Australis* (the southern continent), a huge mythical landmass that was believed to lie somewhere in the Pacific Ocean.

Born in 1565 in Évora, in central Portugal, Pedro Fernández de Quirós became a Spanish subject in 1580, when King Philip II of Spain seized the Portuguese crown. As a result of the union of the two countries, Quirós and other young Portuguese men could find employment in Spain's overseas empire. In the 1580s Quirós emigrated to New Spain (Mexico) and settled in the Pacific port of Acapulco, where he served as a navigator on trading voyages between Acapulco and the Philippine Islands.

MENDAÑA'S EXPEDITION

In 1595 Quirós sailed as chief navigator on a voyage to the Solomon Islands that was led by Álvaro de Mendaña de Neira (born in 1541). Mendaña, as he is usually known, had come upon the islands during an attempt to discover the mythical southern continent, on a voyage that lasted from 1567 to 1569, and had been chosen to return to them to establish a Spanish colony. At that time there was no accurate means of working out a ship's longitude (east-west position). Mendaña underestimated the distance he had traveled on his first voyage because he was unaware that strong currents had carried his ships forward. He was unable to find the Solomon Islands again.

Mendaña tried instead to found a colony on the Santa Cruz Islands, somewhat east of the Solomons. This attempt was a disastrous failure. Rival Spaniards fought and killed each other and treated the islanders with a degree of brutality that Quirós, a deeply religious man, was horrified to witness. (On a later voyage of his own, he told his men that they should treat any peoples they encountered "as fathers do children.") When Mendaña died of malaria on October 18, 1595, Quirós took charge of the expedition and led the survivors to Manila, in the Philippines.

A New Columbus?

Despite Mendaña's failure to find a southern continent, Quirós remained convinced that the continent lay waiting to be discovered and Christianized and that God had chosen him for the task. He believed that Mendaña's expedition had failed because of the wickedness of the Spaniards, who had brought God's punishment upon themselves. In 1600 he traveled to Europe, where he won the backing of Pope Clement VIII and King Philip III of Spain for a new Pacific expedition that he would lead himself.

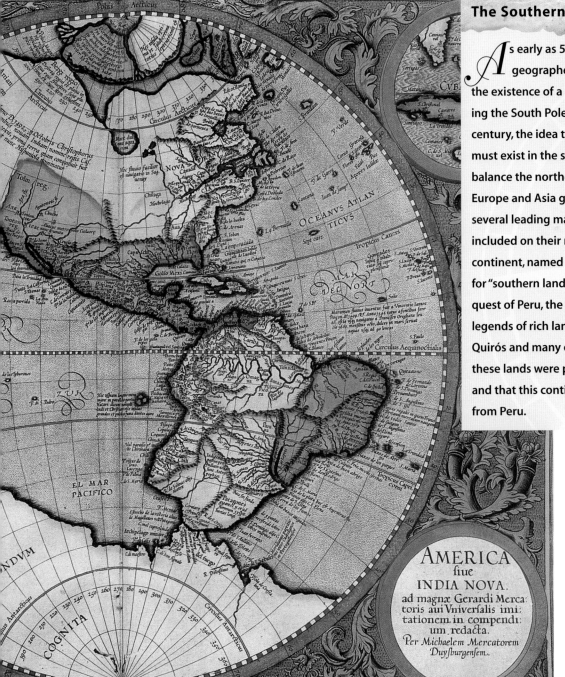

AMERICA
fiue
INDIA NOVA.
ad magnæ Gerardi Merca-
toris aui Vniverfalis imi-
tationem in compendi-
um redacta.
Per Michaelem Mercatorem
Duyfburgenfem.

The Southern Continent

As early as 500 BCE, ancient Greek geographers speculated about the existence of a continent surrounding the South Pole. In the sixteenth century, the idea that a great landmass must exist in the south in order to balance the northern continents of Europe and Asia gathered force, and several leading mapmakers of the time included on their maps a vast southern continent, named *Terra Australis* (Latin for "southern land"). After their conquest of Peru, the Spaniards heard local legends of rich lands lying to the west. Quirós and many others believed that these lands were part of *Terra Australis* and that this continent could not lay far from Peru.

Left **On this 1595 map, drawn by the Flemish cartographer Gerardus Mercator, the huge southern continent is labeled *Terra Australis Nondum Cognita* (southern land not yet known).**

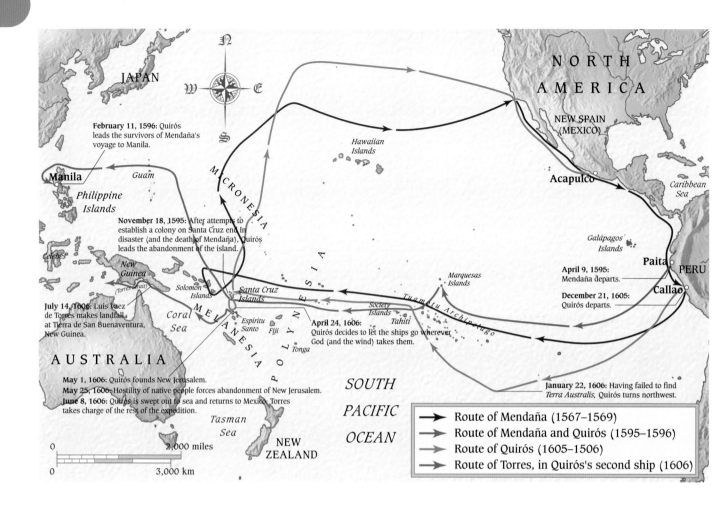

Above **The first European journeys across the South Pacific were problematic because, with no accurate means of determining longitude, explorers had difficulty in distinguishing islands from one another.**

THE PACIFIC VOYAGE

Quirós sailed from Peru on December 21, 1605, with three ships and a crew of three hundred men. After sailing southwest for a month, the ships had still failed to find the southern continent and were forced to alter course in the hope of locating fresh supplies of drinking water. The explorers came upon a number of small islands, but no fresh water was to be found on any of them.

On April 24, 1606, unable to decide in which direction to sail, Quirós gave the order to let the ships go wherever the wind might take them, declaring that "God will guide them as may be right." The wind carried the fleet to the southwest, where a large landmass was sighted on April 29. Quirós believed that he had found the southern continent at last. On landing, he knelt and kissed the ground, saying, "O land, sought for so long, intended to be found by many, and so desired by me!"

In fact, Quirós had reached the island group now called Vanuatu. He named the

---

1565
Pedro Fernández de Quirós is born in Évora, Portugal.

APRIL 9, 1595
Sails with Mendaña to establish a Spanish colony in the Pacific.

SEPTEMBER 21, 1595
Unable to locate the Solomon Islands, Mendaña attempts to establish a colony on the Santa Cruz Islands.

OCTOBER 18, 1595
Following the death of Mendaña, Quirós takes charge of the voyage.

FEBRUARY 11, 1596
Survivors of Mendaña's expedition reach the Philippines.

DECEMBER 21, 1605
Quirós sails from Peru to search for the southern continent.

MAY 1, 1606
Lands on Espíritu Santo (in present-day Vanuatu).

MAY 25, 1606
Abandons colony of New Jerusalem.

JUNE 8, 1606
Quirós's ship is separated from the other two ships.

Quirós knew from bitter experience that the greatest danger on a Pacific crossing was the lack of freshwater. On his 1605–1606 voyage he became the first explorer to carry a machine for converting seawater into freshwater. Seawater was boiled in a container and the steam passed through a tube to a second container, where it condensed back into water. Since the salt was left behind in the first container, the water in the second container was desalinated, or fresh. Quirós's machine made fifty jars of drinking water before its fuel supply ran out.

land Espíritu Santo (Holy Spirit), and attempted to establish a settlement there, which he named New Jerusalem. This project proved to be another failure. Quirós and many of his men fell sick. They were disappointed with Espíritu Santo, which had no gold, a population that was hostile to the Spaniards' attempts to settle the island, and adverse weather and currents that hindered further exploration.

On June 8 the fleet sailed again, in search of a more suitable location for a settlement. When a strong wind swept Quirós's ship out to sea, he abandoned the other two ships and sailed north and east, back to Mexico.

In 1607 Quirós traveled to Spain, where his expedition was judged a failure. He spent the next seven years in poverty, during which time he wrote letter after letter to the Spanish king, begging to be given command of another expedition. In 1614 he was finally given royal approval for another voyage, but in 1615, on his way back to Peru, he died in Panama, in Central America.

November 23, 1606
Quirós reaches Acapulco, in Mexico.

1607
Returns to Spain.

1615
Having secured royal approval for another voyage, dies in Panama on his way back to Peru.

Above **Philip II of Spain made himself king of Portugal in 1580, when the direct line of the Portuguese royal family died out. He based his claim on the fact that his mother was a Portuguese princess.**

SEE ALSO

• Provisioning • Southern Continent • Spain

RALEIGH, WALTER

THE ENGLISH WRITER AND EXPLORER Walter Raleigh (1554–1618) spent many years in the service of Queen Elizabeth I (reigned 1558–1603). On her behalf Raleigh organized and funded three expeditions to set up colonies in North America. Although these settlements were ultimately unsuccessful, they laid the foundation for future English colonization of North America. On two expeditions of his own to South America, Raleigh searched in vain for El Dorado, the legendary golden city.

Below **Although he never visited North America, Walter Raleigh was instrumental in the English colonization of that continent.**

THE LOST COLONY

Walter Raleigh never visited North America himself, perhaps because Queen Elizabeth I, who considered Raleigh one of her favorite courtiers, was unwilling to allow him to leave court. However, he organized and helped to fund three expeditions to found a settlement there. The aim of the first expedition, in 1584, was to locate a site for a future colony. The expeditionary party identified Roanoke Island, off the coast of present-day North Carolina.

The second expedition returned to Roanoke Island in 1585, under the command of Raleigh's cousin, Richard Grenville. Grenville left 107 men under Ralph Lane at Roanoke and returned to England for more supplies. Queen Elizabeth I, known as the Virgin Queen, agreed that the newly claimed territory should be named Virignia in her honor. Meanwhile, on Roanoke, Lane tried to establish food supplies for the settlers and began exploring the surrounding coastline. Two members of the expedition—John White, an artist, and Thomas Harriot, a mathematician—made the earliest surviving maps of Virginia.

When the great English navigator Francis Drake visited the settlement in the spring of 1586, he found the colonists starving and shipped them back to Plymouth. The following year, John White transported 117 new English settlers to Roanoke Island. When

Above **Raleigh's cousin, Richard Grenville (1542–1591), took the first English colonists to Virginia in 1585. He died a hero in 1591 after leading a single ship with a crew of 190 in a fifteen-hour battle against fifteen Spanish galleons.**

New Plants from the New World

When Christopher Columbus reached the New World, tobacco was among the gifts that he was given by the Native Americans. He was unimpressed by the strange dried leaves and threw them away. In the early sixteenth century the use of tobacco began to spread among Europeans, especially sailors. Tobacco was thought to have many medicinal properties, including the ability to cure bad breath and cancer. Walter Raleigh made the smoking of tobacco fashionable in English society. He used a long clay pipe, thought to have been invented by Ralph Lane. Raleigh is also credited with introducing potato cultivation to Europe; he planted potatoes from Virginia on his estate in Ireland in 1589.

White returned to the island three years later, no trace of the colonists could be found.

White searched for the missing colonists, but when a hurricane damaged his ships, he was forced to return to England. Later explorers also attempted to trace the Roanoke settlers. In 1709 John Lawson spent time among the Hatteras Indians in North Carolina. Lawson believed the Hatteras were descended from the missing colonists, but there is no evidence to support his belief. The mystery of the lost colony remains unsolved.

1554
Walter Raleigh is born at Hayes Barton, in southwestern England.

1584
Raleigh's first expedition to North America identifies Roanoke Island as a site for a settlement.

1585
Under Richard Grenville, Raleigh's second expedition to North America builds a settlement at Roanoke Island.

1586
The starving settlers are shipped back to England by Francis Drake.

1587
John White leads a second attempt to settle Roanoke Island, which also fails.

1595
Sailing up the Orinoco River in Venezuela, Raleigh searches for the legendary golden city of El Dorado.

1603
Falls from favor at court and is imprisoned in the Tower of London.

1616
Is released and sets out for the Americas once more. When his men attack a Spanish settlement, the Spanish ambassador demands Raleigh's execution.

1618
Raleigh returns to England and is beheaded in London.

THE SEARCH FOR EL DORADO

Between 1584 and 1590 Antonio de Berrio, a Spanish explorer, had led three expeditions up the Orinoco River, in present-day Venezuela, searching fruitlessly for El Dorado, a fabled city of gold. In 1595, using Berrio's reports of his voyages, Raleigh led his own fleet of four ships up the Orinoco. During a monthlong struggle upstream, Raleigh found no trace of the golden city.

In 1603 Elizabeth I died. The new monarch, King James I, did not favor Raleigh, whom James arrested and accused of treason. Raleigh spent thirteen years imprisoned in the Tower of London. Freed in 1616, he returned to South America. During this last expedition his men attacked a Spanish settlement, and the Spanish ambassador in London demanded Raleigh's head. When Raleigh returned to London in 1618, he was indeed beheaded.

In his report of his 1595 Orinoco journey, Raleigh includes the following passage from an earlier Spanish account of the king of El Dorado:

All the vessels of his house, table, and kitchen, were of gold and silver. . . . He had in his wardrobe hollow statues of gold which seemed giants, and the figures in proportion and bigness of all the beasts, birds, trees, and herbs, that the earth bringeth forth; and of all the fishes that the sea or waters of his kingdom breedeth . . . there was nothing in his country whereof he had not the counterfeit in gold. . . . [He had] a garden of pleasure . . . which had all kinds of garden-herbs, flowers, and trees of gold and silver; an invention and magnificence till then never seen.

Walter Raleigh, *The Discoverie of Guiana*

SEE ALSO
- Belalcázar, Sebastián de • Drake, Francis
- Great Britain • Hakluyt, Richard
- Record Keeping

RECORD KEEPING

WHETHER ON PAPYRUS, CLAY TABLET, CAMCORDER, or handheld computer, explorers from ancient times to modern have always kept records of the routes they followed, the people and natural phenomena they encountered, and the feelings they experienced on their journeys. Expedition data is not only of use to other explorers: for specialists it can provide new insights into the climate, maritime conditions, landscape, wildlife, and culture of unfamiliar territory. The publication of expedition records brings these insights to the attention of a wider public audience.

THE PURPOSE OF RECORD KEEPING

Explorers maintain a detailed record of their route for a number of reasons. They may need proof that the journey they claim to have made actually took place. Maps, navigational charts, and the ship's log allow future travelers to follow the same route. For countries seeking to build an overseas empire, maps were the basis of claims to ownership of any new lands explorers reached. Some countries, including England and France, assembled all the data gathered during journeys of exploration in a particular place. The records were then made available to scientists and military personnel, who might in turn use the records in planning future exploration of the lands in question.

Organizing an expedition is expensive, and the expedition's sponsors (those who pay for it) need to be sure that their money has been well spent. Logs, journals, and financial accounts record the successes achieved, the problems encountered, and the contribution made by different members of the expedition party. This information can then be used in the planning of future journeys. The records of modern explorers often serve as a basis for the book, lecture tour, or television program that will provide an income to fund the next venture.

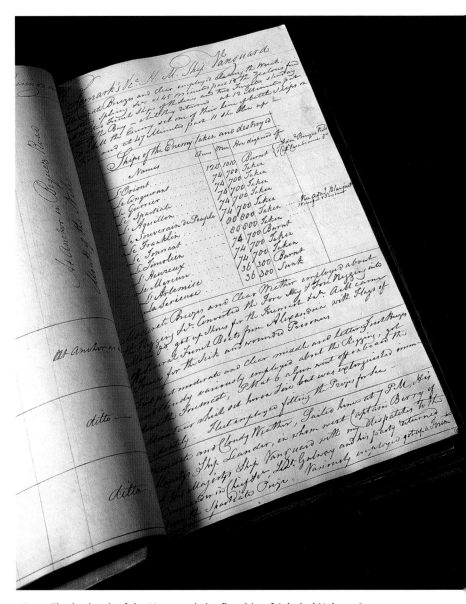

Above **The logbook of the *Vanguard*, the flagship of Admiral Nelson. Among many other things, the logbook lists the French ships captured or sunk during the battle at Abukir Bay, Egypt, in 1798.**

Above **The polar explorer Robert F. Scott kept detailed notes of his final expedition to the South Pole (1911–1912), which ended in the death of Scott and his men.**

RECORD KEEPING IN EARLY CIVILIZATIONS

Historians know of the exploration undertaken by ancient peoples, such as the Babylonians, Egyptians, and Phoenicians, because many of the records these peoples kept of their expeditions still survive. For example, the explorer Hanno (c. 530–470 BCE), who came from the North African city of Carthage, had his record of his journey down the western coast of Africa inscribed on a clay tablet. His account is known as the *Periplus* (literally, "sailing around"). One evening, passing near to the coast of Sierra Leone, Hanno saw a volcano. He recorded a "land at night covered with flames. And in the midst there was one lofty fire, greater than the rest, which seemed to touch the stars. By day this was seen to be a very high mountain, called the Chariot of the Gods." Hanno's volcano is usually associated with Mount Kakulima, in Guinea.

CLASSIC WRITTEN ACCOUNTS

The events and observations explorers record daily in logs and journals are often developed, after the completion of the expedition, into narrative accounts. One of the greatest explorers of medieval times was the North African Muslim traveler Ibn Battutah (1304–1377). Ibn Battutah journeyed throughout the entire Muslim world to places as far apart as Tombouctou (in Mali, West Africa), Spain, Mecca (in Saudi Arabia), the Russian steppes, and China. His records, collected in an account known as *Rihlah* (Travels), detail the customs, cultural particularities, and natural resources of the territories he visited.

Marco Polo, Christopher Columbus, James Cook, and a great many other explorers turned their diaries and logs into travel books. Marco Polo's account, usually known as *Il Milione*, is one of the most highly esteemed travel books ever published. Publication of explorers' records helped to broaden people's understanding of different cultures. However, not every explorer applied scientific rigor to record keeping. Many allowed their imagination to enliven their material, and several travel books contain records of such fanciful phenomena as two-headed monsters and trees bearing live lambs rather than fruit.

CLASSIC VISUAL RECORDS

Many explorers illustrated their written records. Christopher Columbus, for instance, included rough sketches of Caribbean landscapes in his accounts. Official artists joined many of the great sea voyages launched between the fifteenth and eighteenth centuries. The artist John White, for example, traveled on the expeditions to North America organized by Walter Raleigh between 1584 and 1587. White's extraordinary sketches of the Algonquian inhabitants of North Carolina vividly depict the appearance and daily life of these Native Americans before the arrival of European settlers in large numbers led to the destruction of Algonquian culture.

John White *DIED C. 1593*

*I*n 1577 the English painter John White accompanied Martin Frobisher's Baffin Island expedition and sketched the native Inuit. In 1585, as part of the first Roanoke expedition, White sketched flora and fauna and Native American life. His paintings, significant records of a culture that was new to Europeans, illustrated Thomas Harriot's *Briefe and True Report of the New Found Land of Virginia* (1588).

John White returned to Roanoke in July 1587 with a party that included his daughter and her husband. Their daughter, Virginia Dare, was the first child born in America of English parents. Nine days after his granddaughter's birth, White left for England. War with Spain prevented him from returning to Roanoke until 1590, by which time there was no trace of his granddaughter, her parents, or any of the colonists.

Above As he explored and mapped the area around Roanoke Island, John White recorded the appearance and everyday life of such Alqonquians as this man, who is dressed and painted for hunting.

Right **During her solo trip around the world in 2002, the British yatchswoman Emma Richards made use of a range of instruments to plan and record her journey.**

MODERN RECORD KEEPING

By the beginning of the twentieth century, photographic equipment was portable enough to be taken on expeditions. The polar exploration parties led by the English explorers Robert F. Scott (1910–1912) and Ernest Shackleton (1914–1916) both included photographers. Indeed, the reverence with which both explorers are remembered is due in part to the unforgettable photos taken by Herbert Ponting, who went with Scott, and Frank Hurley, who went with Shackelton. (Nevertheless, perhaps as a backup, both Scott and Shackelton also took sketch artists).

By the end of the twentieth century, explorers were using small, lightweight digital recording devices, such as laptop computers, PDAs (personal digital assistants), and digital cameras. Since vast amounts of digital data can be stored on a tiny microchip, exhaustive records of an expedition are now easily kept. Yet one downpour can render any electrical equipment useless, and many modern explorers still resort to pen and paper.

The process of making records publicly available is also becoming increasingly

Digital Camcorder

*D*igital camcorders are extremely important record-keeping tools for explorers. Small enough to be held in one hand, they record high-quality and accurate moving images and sound that can then be transmitted across the world instantly via a satellite phone link. Even the smallest camcorder can record up to a million and a half different shades of light.

simple. With a satellite phone, an explorer can send up-to-the-minute reports and images to a Web site, where they can be accessed by anyone in the world with an internet connection. Unmanned devices exploring the farthest reaches of space record data using sonar, radar, infrared, and other imaging techniques. These records are stored digitally and easily transmitted to scientists for analysis.

SEE ALSO
- Columbus, Christopher
- Communication Devices • Hanno of Carthage
- Ibn Battutah • Mapmaking • Native Peoples
- Navigation • Photography • Polo, Marco
- Raleigh, Walter • Shackleton, Ernest Henry

REMOTE SENSING

REMOTE SENSING IS THE PROCESS BY WHICH a remote device—that is, one controlled from a distance—gathers scientific data about an object or a place. Remote devices are especially useful for undertaking lengthy explorations of the earth from the air; a vast amount of valuable data may be gathered without placing human life in danger.

EARLY DEVELOPMENTS

Remote sensing dates back to the mid-nineteenth century, when cameras attached to balloons took photographs of the earth from the air. Tethered to the ground, the balloons could photograph only the immediate surrounding area. Around the beginning of the twentieth century, a group of people from Bavaria, in southern Germany, used homing pigeons to carry cameras that were programmed to take a photograph every few seconds. However, this method of mapping the earth was somewhat haphazard.

AERIAL PHOTOGRAPHY

Remote sensing was revolutionized by the invention of powered flight. During World War I (1914–1918), pilots on reconnaissance missions (fact-finding flights) took photographs to record the topography of enemy-held territory or the strength and location of enemy defenses. Aerial photography became more sophisticated during World War II (1939–1945) with advances in camera technology and photointerpretation (the identification of objects in photographs).

THE ELECTROMAGNETIC SPECTRUM

All objects with a temperature above absolute zero (–273°C) emit, absorb, and reflect many different forms of wave energy. The range of all known energy, the electromagnetic spectrum, encompasses both visible forms (light waves) and invisible forms (infrared, ultraviolet, and radio waves). Aerial photography captures on film the waves visible to the human eye. After World War II, instruments developed to capture nonvisible wave energy emitted by objects greatly extended the range of vision of scientists.

Below **The European Remote-Sensing Satellite (ERS-1) was tested in Toulouse, France, before its launch in 1991. It spent nine years studying the world's oceans.**

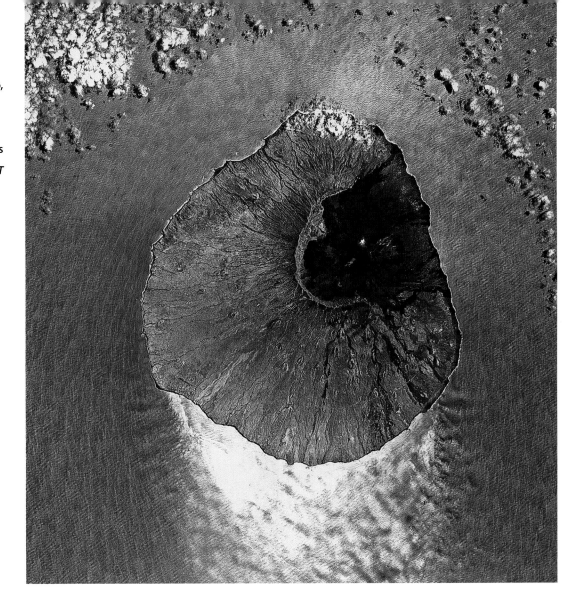

Right **This infrared satellite image of Fogo, one of the volcanic Cape Verde Islands in the Atlantic Ocean, was taken by a French *SPOT* satellite. Bare ground appears dark grey, water is blue, green vegetation is red, and clouds are white. (*"SPOT"* is an acronym for "*système pour l'observation de la terre*," which means "earth-observation system.")**

Nonphotographic remote-sensing devices can be used to record what the earth's surface looks like through dense cloud cover, haze, dust, darkness, and even layers of sand. Such devices provide data that has been invaluable to geographers, geologists, soil scientists, farmers, foresters, and cartographers around the world.

MAPPING THE EARTH

The first satellite designed specifically as a remote-sensing platform was the Earth Resources Technology Satellite, later named *Landsat I*. Launched in 1972, the satellite carried a four-channel multispectral scanner that recorded four different wavelengths simultaneously.

1840s
Cameras attached to balloons are used to take aerial photographs of a fixed area.

c. 1900
Cameras attached to pigeons take sequences of aerial photographs of Bavaria.

1903
Wilbur and Orville Wright make the first successful aeroplane flight.

1914–1918
World War I combatants take aerial photographs of one another's territory.

1942–1945
The U.S. Navy's extensive use of aerial photography in the Pacific war zone contributes to the Allied victory in World War II.

1960
The first weather satellite, *TIROS 1,* uses remote-sensing equipment to monitor the weather.

1972
Landsat 1 is launched, with a video camera and multispectral scanner on board.

1976
Lageos 1 helps scientists to measure movements of the earth's surface.

Remote-sensing satellites provide a wide variety of information about the earth. They monitor environmental problems, such as oil spills, keep track of fish stocks, assess crop and forest conditions by measuring crop densities and plant temperatures, and even help prospectors to find oil and mineral deposits beneath the earth's surface. Thermal monitoring of volcanoes has been used to identify volcanic activity and to observe the progress of lava flows and eruption clouds. In 1997 this type of remote sensing gave the first indication of an eruption of the faraway Okmok volcano in Alaska.

Remote sensing enables very accurate mapping of the earth and allows scientists and cartographers to identify changes in the world's coastlines, such as those caused by the melting of the polar ice caps. Remote sensing is also used to map the hidden depths of the world's oceans, until now the least-explored areas of the earth.

The Hole in the Ozone Layer

The ozone layer is a layer of gas in the upper atmosphere that envelops the earth and absorbs most of the sun's harmful ultraviolet radiation—and thus protects all living things on the earth from certain death. Scientists from the British Antarctic Survey began monitoring the thickness of the ozone layer above the Antarctic in 1957. They discovered that, during certain months of the year, the ozone layer was thinning dramatically. However, it was not until the NASA satellite *Nimbus 7* was launched in October 1978 that images of the hole in the ozone layer could be recorded with a remote-sensing device called a total ozone mapping spectrometer (TOMS). It is now hoped that a reduction in the use of chloroflourocarbons (CFCs), the gases that damage the ozone layer, will allow it to repair itself.

1978
During a 98-day operation, *Seasat,* launched to study oceanic and atmospheric phenomena, provides the first high-resolution radar images of the earth's surface.

1978
Nimbus 7 observes changes in the thickness of the earth's ozone layer.

1999
Instruments carried aboard *Landsat 7* measure changes in the surface of the earth and the shape of its coastlines.

Above **This TOMS (total ozone mapping spectrometer) image, taken on October 3, 1999, shows the hole in the ozone layer (pale blue) above Antarctica (dark blue).**

SEE ALSO

• Aviation • Communication Devices • Earth
• Satellites • Spacecraft • Weather Forecasting

RICCI, MATTEO

MATTEO RICCI (1552–1610), AN ITALIAN MISSIONARY, traveled to China in 1582, a time when it was almost impossible for foreigners to enter that country. Having gained the respect and trust of the Chinese by learning the Chinese language, Ricci lived in China for almost thirty years. His books, written in Chinese, introduced many European ideas and scientific developments to China, while his letters home brought knowledge of the East to Europe.

Above **In 1595 Ricci took to wearing the silk robes and tall black hat of a mandarin, a Chinese scholar and official.**

From an early age, Ricci showed a remarkable ability to remember information. After reading a page of a book just once, he could repeat it word for word. In Rome he learned to improve his memory skills still further, using a method invented by Quintilian, a Roman writer who lived in the first century CE. According to Quintilian's method, Ricci first converted thoughts into striking mental pictures. Next he organized these pictures in his mind by placing them in the rooms and corridors of an imaginary building. To retrieve a thought, he would imagine himself walking through the building until he found the image that corresponded to the thought. Ricci later described this method as "building a memory palace."

In 1577 Ricci decided to become a Christian missionary. The following year he sailed to Goa, a Portuguese colony on the western coast of India, where he trained to become a priest. In 1582 he traveled to the Portuguese enclave of Macao, on the Chinese coast.

EDUCATION OF A MISSIONARY
Born into a noble family from Macerata, in eastern Italy, Matteo Ricci was educated by Jesuit priests and in 1571 joined their order as a novice (trainee). He studied at the Jesuit college in Rome, one of the finest educational establishments in Europe.

LEARNING CHINESE
For many years the Jesuits in Macao had been trying to get permission to enter China in order to spread Christianity. Many Chinese considered foreigners to be ignorant and uncultured, and fearing that European influence was potentially dangerous to the

The Jesuits

Jesuits are members of the Society of Jesus, a religious order that was founded in 1540 by Ignatius Loyola, a Spaniard. The Society of Jesus was set up in response to the religious changes that were taking place in Europe during the sixteenth century. Large numbers of Christians in northern and central Europe had broken away from the Roman Catholic Church and established their own Protestant churches. Loyola and his followers hoped not only to strengthen the Roman Catholic Church in Europe but also to engage in missionary work that would carry Roman Catholicism throughout the world.

Left While he lived, Ignatius Loyola (1491–1556), founder of the Jesuits, never sat for a portrait. This portrait was painted immediately after Loyola's death by Jacopino del Conte, an Italian artist.

stability and order of their society, the Chinese had always refused the Jesuits' requests. Although they had allowed the Portuguese to settle in Macao for trading purposes, they had walled off the port on the landward side to keep the *fan kwei* ("foreign devils") out.

Alessandro Valignano, Ricci's superior, believed that the only way that Europeans would find acceptance among the Chinese would be by learning their language—an extremely difficult challenge for a European. In 1579 Valignano had given a Jesuit named Michele Ruggieri the task of learning Chinese, but Ruggieri had made little progress. In contrast, Ricci, with his remarkable memory, learned rapidly. In three months, he knew more Chinese than Ruggieri had mastered in three years.

RICCI IN CHINA

In 1583 Ricci and Ruggieri entered China. Hoping to be accepted into Chinese society, they dressed in Chinese clothes. At Chaoking, the local governor, Wang-P'an, gave the men permission to stay and build a house, on condition that they agreed to live as Chinese and become subjects of the Chinese emperor.

Ricci spent his first years in Chaoking learning as much as he could about the Chinese way of life. In 1585, in a letter to a friend in Italy, he wrote, "I have become a Chinaman." He was so eager to be accepted that he later said that, if it had been possible, he would have changed the shape of his eyes and nose in order to look more Chinese.

Ricci knew that the Chinese were proud of their ancient civilization. To win converts to his religion, he needed to show that his own civilization was also worthy of respect. He gave clocks and astronomical instruments produced in Europe to Chinese officials. To demonstrate European geographical learning, he produced a Chinese translation of the world map drawn in 1570 by Abraham Ortelius.

Success in Chinese society depended in no small part on having a good memory. China was ruled, on behalf of the emperor, by scholar-officials—who obtained their jobs and promotions by passing lengthy written exams. Ricci displayed his memory skills by having people write down hundreds of Chinese letters. To onlookers' amazement he

would read the letters once and then repeat the sequence accurately, forward and backward. Ricci's Chinese acquaintances begged him to teach them his memory system, and in

---

1552
Matteo Ricci is born at Macerata in Italy.

1571
Enters the Society of Jesus in Rome.

1577
Decides to become a missionary and travels to Portugal to find a ship to take him to Asia.

1578
Sails from Portugal to Goa in India.

1580
Becomes a priest.

1582
Travels to Macao.

1583
Enters China and settles in Chaoking.

1584
Produces a map of the world in Chinese.

1589–1601
Travels around southern and eastern China, settling for short periods in Su-chou, Nanking and Nan-ch'ang.

1601
Settles in Beijing.

1609
Writes an account in Italian of his time in China.

1610
Dies and is buried in Beijing.

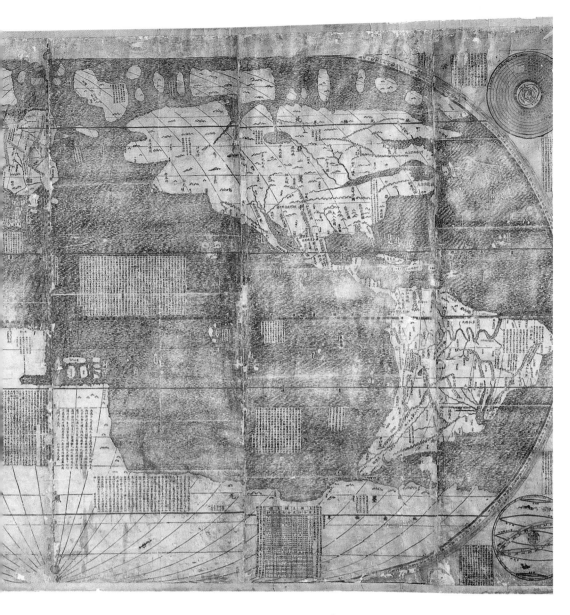

The following passage is from an introduction, written by a Chinese friend, to one of Ricci's books. Li Madou was the name given to Ricci by the Chinese:

I have come to know Li Madou. He is a man from the Far West, with a full beard and few words. I know all his writings and am convinced that he is truly a remarkable man. Because they are separated by a distance . . . equal to that between heaven and earth, the Western Countries and the Middle Kingdom [China] could not communicate. But now Li Madou has begun to bring them together. After travelling through hundreds of kingdoms and cities, only the Middle Flower [China] has pleased him.

Quoted in Vincent Cronin, *The Wise Man from the West*

1596 he wrote a book in Chinese explaining his technique. He also wrote short works in which he explained Christianity in terms that made sense to the Chinese.

From 1601 Ricci lived in the imperial capital, Beijing, where he wrote several more books in Chinese. By the time of his death in 1610, he had converted around two thousand Chinese to Christianity. He had also done much to modify the prevailing Chinese prejudice against foreigners.

SEE ALSO

• Missions

RUSSIA

RUSSIA'S CONTRIBUTION TO WORLD EXPLORATION dates from around 1600, when merchants seeking to exploit the natural resources of Siberia pioneered the first routes east across the Ural Mountains and from there south into central Asia. By 1800 Russian expeditions had penetrated Asia and crossed the Pacific Ocean to North America. During the first half of the twentieth century, Russian explorers achieved significant landmarks in Arctic exploration, and since the 1950s Russians have played a pioneering role in the exploration of space.

Below **A 1776 engraving of an Ostyak (a native of western Siberia) hunting ermine. Fur trappers were among the first Russians to push east into the Siberian wilderness.**

FRONTIERSMEN AND EXPLORERS

At the beginning of the seventeenth century, the Russian population was concentrated in the European (western) part of the country. To the east, beyond the Ural Mountains, lay Siberia, a vast unexplored wilderness. The first Russians to explore Siberia were hunters seeking valuable animal furs. Russian *promyshlenniki* (frontiersmen) probably reached Cape Chelyuskin, the northernmost part of the Eurasian landmass, around 1620. In 1638 Ivan Moskvitin reached the Pacific shore of the Sea of Okhotsk, and Semyon Dezhnyov discovered the strait separating Asia and America in 1648 (though his voyage report was not discovered until 1736). As they spread eastward, the Russians built fortresses to protect their interests. These grew into Siberian cities, such as Tomsk (founded in 1604), Krasnoyarsk (1628), and Yakutsk (1632).

Shortly before his death in 1725, Czar Peter the Great gave orders for a great scientific and military expedition to the Russian Far East, to be led by the Danish commander Vitus Bering. On the first expedition known to have crossed the sea that separates Russia from North America (now named the Bering Strait), Bering reached Saint Lawrence Island, Alaska, on August 10, 1728.

Expeditions under Otto von Kotzebue from 1815 to 1818 and Ferdinand Petrovich von Wrangel between 1820 and 1824 continued the job of surveying and mapping Russia's new lands and coastline in the eastern Arctic. In 1901 Admiral S. O. Makarov reached Spitsbergen and Novaya Zemlya in his icebreaking ship *Yermak*.

Russians in America

Russian merchants were attracted to Alaska by reports of the vast numbers of sea otters in the region. The sea otter was especially prized for its thick, warm fur. By 1765 forty Russian companies were working in Alaska. They built bases, used the local Unanga people as hunters, and handed over one-tenth of their furs to the Russian government as tax. The empress Catherine the Great (reigned 1762–1796) used some of this wealth to sponsor scientific expeditions to Alaska under Petr Krenitsyn (1768), Mikhail Levashov (1768–1770), and the British naval officer Joseph Billings (1790). Until the mid-nineteenth century, many Russians hunted and traded in the far north of the American continent. This activity declined after 1867, when the United States purchased the Russian Empire's stake in Alaska for 7.2 million dollars.

Right **During the long reign of Catherine II, also known as Catherine the Great, Russians explored northern Siberia and Alaska. Catherine was eager to have these areas systematically mapped.**

Other Russians explored the southern edges of the Russian Far East. In 1643 Kurbat Ivanov reached Lake Baikal, in southern Siberia. In the late nineteenth century the geographer Nikolay Przhevalsky made five expeditions through central Asia, during which he traveled to Ussuri (near the Chinese border), Mongolia, and Tibet.

Russians also took part in the exploration of Antarctica. Fabian Gottlieb von Bellingshausen led a Russian naval expedition to the southern continent between 1819 and 1821. Bellingshausen's expedition made the first recorded sighting of Antarctica in January 1820 and also discovered many uncharted islands and atolls in the Southern Ocean.

Arctic Exploration in the Soviet Period

During the Soviet period (1917–1991), exploration offered the government an important opportunity to display the scientific progress that the country was making. In 1932 the Soviet icebreaker *Sibiryakov* became the first ship to complete the Northeast Passage in a single season. Not only did this voyage constitute a landmark in the history of exploration, it also opened up the Arctic Sea as a viable route for cargo ships transporting minerals from Siberia to the factories of European Russia. In 1977 the nuclear-powered icebreaker *Artika* smashed a route through the ice to the North Pole.

Soviet explorers also pioneered the use of drifting research stations. In 1937 Ivan Papanin, Eugeny Fedorov, Peter Shirshov, and Ernest Krenkel set up a scientific base called *North Pole 1* on an ice floe (a large flat mass of drifting sea ice). Carried for more than 1,600 miles (2,600 km), the men made important discoveries about the polar climate, the depth of the ocean, and Arctic currents. By the end of the twentieth century, more than thirty drifting research stations had been established in the Russian Arctic.

Below **A tent surrounded by deep snow, part of the Soviet scientific base** *North Pole 1,* **which drifted through the Arctic in 1937.**

1638	1725–1730	1820	1937	1948
Ivan Moskvitin reaches the Sea of Okhotsk.	Vitus Bering makes his first Siberia expedition.	Bellingshausen makes the first recorded sighting of Antarctica.	The research station *North Pole 1* is established on a drifting ice floe.	Russian pilots become the first to land aircraft at the North Pole.
1648	**1733–1741**	**1901**		**1957**
Semyon Dezhnyov reaches the eastern coast of the Eurasian landmass.	Bering's Great Northern Expedition maps the northern and eastern coasts of Russia.	Admiral Makarov reaches Spitsbergen and Novaya Zemlya.		*Sputnik 1,* the first spacecraft to orbit the earth, is launched.

SPACE EXPLORATION

The Soviet Union launched the first spacecraft to orbit the earth, *Sputnik 1*, in October 1957. The Russians were also the first to send a person into space: in April 1961, Yury Gagarin, a young flight officer, completed one orbit of the earth during a 108-minute flight. The first woman in space was also Russian; in June 1963 Valentina Tereshkova orbited the earth forty-eight times in *Vostok 6*.

In February 1986 the Soviet Union launched *Mir* (the Russian word for "peace"), an orbiting station that was used as a permanent space laboratory. Dr. Valeri Polyakov set a new record for the length of time a person had spent in space when he remained aboard *Mir* from January 1994 to March 1995.

Long-Distance Aviators

In June 1937 the Soviet aviator Valery Chkalov piloted his single-engine plane from Moscow to Vancouver, Washington, via the North Pole. His flight took over sixty-two hours and covered more than 5,500 miles (8,850 km). Chkalov's record was broken within a month when Mikhail Gromov flew 6,300 miles (10,140 km) from Moscow via the North Pole to San Jacinto, California. In 1948 three Soviet planes carrying scientific equipment touched down on the ice at 90° north latitude—they were the first planes to land at the exact location of the North Pole.

Originally built to last only five years, *Mir* was finally retired from service in March 2001; after entering the earth's atmosphere, it crashed in a fiery ball into the Pacific Ocean.

1961
Yury Gagarin becomes the first man in space.

1977
The nuclear-powered icebreaker *Artika* reaches the North Pole.

1986–2001
Mir is used as a space laboratory by sixty-two astronauts from different countries.

SEE ALSO

- Astronauts • Bellinghausen, Fabian Gottlieb von
- Bering, Vitus Jonassen
- Gagarin, Yury • Northeast Passage
- Przhevalsky, Nikolay • Satellites
- Space Exploration

SACAGAWEA

A SHOSHONE WOMAN BORN AROUND 1790, Sacagawea played a key role in the Lewis and Clark expedition, which explored the Louisiana Territory of the United States between 1804 and 1806. Sacagawea's presence helped to establish Lewis and Clark's peaceful intentions toward the Native American peoples they met. As a result, the expedition received badly needed aid on several occasions. Most authorities agree that Sacagawea died in 1812.

Below **This sculpture of Sacagawea (whose true appearance is a matter of conjecture) stands in Boise, Idaho.**

LIFE BEFORE THE EXPEDITION

Little is known for certain of Sacagawea's life before she met Meriwether Lewis and William Clark in the winter of 1804. She was born, probably in 1790, to a chief of the Lemhi branch of the Shoshone people. Her group lived in the northern Rocky Mountains, near present-day Lemhi, Idaho. In about 1800 a band of Hidatsa—a neighboring group of Native Americans—attacked Sacagawea's people while they were hunting buffalo on the northern Great Plains. The Hidatsa carried the ten-year-old girl off to their village and gave her the name Sacagawea, which means "bird woman." Around 1804 a Canadian fur trader named Toussaint Charbonneau, who was living with the Hidatsa, purchased Sacagawea and married her.

JOURNEY TO THE PACIFIC

In 1804 Lewis and Clark set out on their epic journey from Missouri to the Pacific Ocean. They met Charbonneau and Sacagawea

---

c. 1790
Sacagawea is born into a group of Shoshone people.

1800
Is captured by Hidatsa raiders.

1804
Is purchased from the Hidatsa by Toussaint Charbonneau; both are recruited by Lewis and Clark.

SPRING 1805
Sacagawea's son is born; the Lewis and Clark expedition sets out from Fort Mandan.

NOVEMBER 1805
The expedition reaches the Pacific Ocean.

1806
Charbonneau and Sacagawea part from Lewis and Clark on the return journey.

1809
Sacagawea possibly travels with Charbonneau to Saint Louis.

c. 1812
Dies.

when they halted for the winter near Hidatsa territory on the Great Bend of the Missouri River, near present-day Bismarck, North Dakota. When Lewis and Clark hired Charbonneau as an interpreter and cook, they decided to take Sacagawea with them as well, anticipating that, as a speaker of Shoshone, she would be useful to them when they crossed Shoshone land.

On February 11, 1805, Sacagawea gave birth to a boy. Eight weeks later Lewis, Clark, and their party of more than thirty people set out again for the West. Charbonneau and Sacagawea—together with their newborn son—were part of the group.

Despite the many claims that have been made for Sacagawea's role as a guide on the trip west, those claims are not borne out in Lewis and Clark's journals. She was valuable chiefly as an interpreter rather than as a guide. She also helped by identifying plants that could be used as food or medicine. Perhaps her most important contribution lay simply in her mere presence, which reassured the Native Americans whom Lewis and Clark met on their way that the travelers did not present an immediate threat. As Clark himself wrote, "a woman with a party of men is a token of peace."

After the Lewis and Clark expedition returned from the Pacific, the leaders paid off Charbonneau but gave Sacagawea nothing for her work. In a letter to Charbonneau, Clark later expressed his regrets for this oversight:

Your woman who accompanied you that long dangerous and fatiguing route to the Pacific Ocean and back, deserved a greater reward for her attention and services on that route than we had in our power to give her.

William Clark, from a letter to Toussaint Charbonneau, August 20, 1806

Below **This book illustration reflects the traditional—but incorrect—view of Sacagawea as a guide for Lewis and Clark.**

SACAJAWEA DIED-APRIL 9, 1884 A GUIDE WITH THE LEWIS AND CLARK EXPEDITION 1805 — 1806 IDENTIFIED 1907 BY REV. J. ROBERTS WHO OFFICIATED AT HER BURIAL

Above **Mythical versions of Sacagawea's life persist. This young Shoshone girl stands at a Wyoming monument dedicated to her ancestor, a woman who died in 1884 and who some claim was Sacagawea. Most historians do not accept this claim.**

On certain occasions, Sacagawea proved indispensable. Early in the trip, she rescued valuable notes and other items from a capsized boat. In August 1805 the party was met by Sacagawea's people in the Rocky Mountains. By that time her brother was chief of their branch of the Shoshone people. Sacagawea's presence made it easier for the party to buy horses. She also proved her worth as a translator on several occasions during the hazardous crossing of the Rocky Mountains.

THE MYSTERY OF HER FATE

The Lewis and Clark expedition reached the Pacific in November 1805. After spending the winter encamped in present-day Oregon, the men began their return journey in March 1806. Charbonneau and Sacagawea left the expedition when they reached the Hidatsa village again, in August 1806.

After a failed attempt to make a living from farming in Missouri, Sacagawea and her husband moved to Fort Manuel, a trading post on the Missouri River. Most historians believe that she died there, probably in 1812. There is, however, an alternative view, according to which Sacagawea outlived her husband and returned to her own people, the Shoshone, and lived among them until her death at the age of almost a hundred.

SEE ALSO

• Lewis and Clark Expedition

SATELLITES

A SATELLITE IS AN OBJECT, NATURAL OR ARTIFICIAL, THAT ORBITS (travels around) a celestial body, usually a planet. Whereas the planet Earth has only a single natural satellite—the Moon—other planets in the solar system have several moons (although Venus and Mercury have none). Artificial satellites, transported into space and released into orbit around the earth at a predetermined altitude, serve a number of scientific purposes.

HOW SATELLITES STAY IN ORBIT

All objects in the universe, from particles to planets, possess gravity, a fundamental natural force that pulls one object toward another. The larger an object is, the greater its gravity. The pull of a planet's gravitational force is strong enough to attract a satellite and keep it from hurtling off into space.

Forces other than the gravitational pull of a planet govern the movement of a satellite. The moon, for example, has its own momentum, a natural movement that pulls it away from the earth. Acting against the earth's gravity, the moon's momentum prevents it from crashing into the earth. Throughout the solar system, a combination of interacting forces keeps celestial bodies in orbit around one another and the whole system in orbit around the sun. This series of perpetual circular motions has been compared poetically to a dance.

Artificial satellites also need momentum, strong enough to act against the planet's gravitational pull and prevent them from crashing into the surface but not so strong as to propel them beyond the reach of that gravitational pull. A satellite must be launched at precisely the correct orbital velocity to give it the momentum to stay in orbit. A satellite at an altitude of 150 miles (242 km), for example, must travel at about seventeen thousand miles per hour (27,359 km/h).

Below **This image of Jupiter and five of its natural satellites was created using data gathered by *Voyager* spacecraft in 1979. The moons pictured are Ganymede (left), Europa (center), Io (right), Callisto (far right), and Leda (the rocky foreground).**

The First Satellites

In 1687 the English physicist Sir Isaac Newton (1642–1727) first suggested the possibility of placing an artificial satellite into orbit. However, it was some 270 years before his idea became a reality. During the cold war, a period of ideological and political conflict that lasted from 1945 to 1991, the two opposing superpowers, the United States and the Soviet Union, competed in the so-called space race. On October 4, 1957, the Soviet Union won the race to launch the first artificial satellite into orbit. *Sputnik 1* was a metal ball that weighed 183 pounds (83.6 kg) and carried a thermometer, a battery, and two radio transmitters. Attached to *Sputnik 1* were four antennae that successfully transmitted radio signals back to earth. Although the radio signals ceased after twenty-three days, when the satellite's battery ran out, *Sputnik 1* remained in orbit for three months. Eventually the satellite slowed, and as gravity gradually pulled it back toward the earth, it burned up on entering the atmosphere.

Barely a month later, on January 31, 1958, the United States launched *Explorer 1*. This first U.S. satellite studied cosmic phenomena as well as monitoring its own temperature. *Explorer 1* helped to detect the Van Allen radiation belt, zones of highly charged particles trapped in the magnetosphere, a high-altitude layer of the earth's atmosphere. In October 1958 NASA (National Aeronautics and Space Administration) was formed to lead U.S. endeavors in the space race.

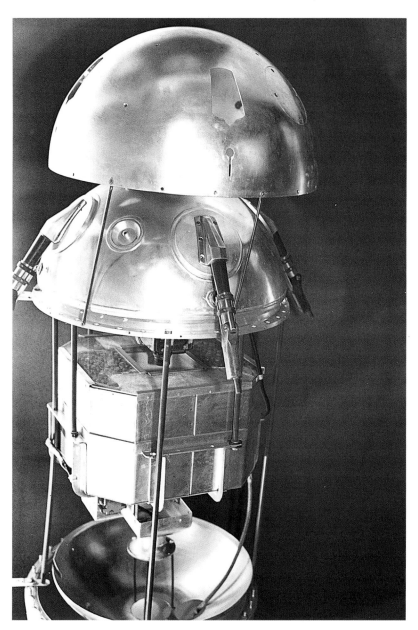

Left **This photograph of *Sputnik 1* shows its various parts separated: when launched, it formed a sphere twenty-three inches (58 cm) in diameter.**

1957
Sputnik 1, the first artificial satellite to orbit the earth, is launched by the Soviet Union.

1958
Explorer 1 is launched by the United States.

1960
NASA launches *TIROS,* the world's first weather satellite.

1962
Telstar 1, the first active communications satellite, is launched by NASA.

1964
Nimbus, the first of a new generation of weather satellites, is launched.

1971
Salyut 1 becomes the world's first manned space station.

1978
The first Global Positioning System (GPS) satellite is launched. *Seasat,* the first satellite devoted to observation of the oceans, begins its mission.

1990
The Hubble Space Telescope (HST) is put into orbit.

1998
The first parts of the International Space Station (ISS) are carried into space on board the space shuttle.

President John F. Kennedy considered the launch of *Telstar I* one of the most significant U.S. achievements in the space race:

The successful firing and subsequent operation of the Telstar communications satellite is an outstanding example of the way in which government and business can cooperate in a most important field of human endeavor. The achievement of the communications satellite . . . throws open to us the vision of an era of international communications. There is no more important field at the present time than communications, and we must grasp the advantages presented to us by the communications satellite to use this medium wisely and effectively to ensure greater understanding among the peoples of the world.

From a statement of July 11, 1962

Satellite Communication

Communications satellites, first developed in the late 1950s, receive a signal transmitted from the earth, amplify the signal, and then beam it back down to a different part of the earth. They enable speedy and accurate communication of data between one part of the world and another. On July 10, 1962, *Telstar 1*, the world's first commercial communications satellite, was launched. Built and operated by the American Telephone and Telegraph Company (AT&T), *Telstar 1* was the first satellite to transmit live telephone conversations and television programs across the Atlantic Ocean.

Above **Engineers prepare *Telstar 1*, the world's first commercial communications satellite, for launch.**

Above **This photograph was taken seconds after the Hubble Space Telescope (HST) was lifted from the payload bay of the space shuttle *Discovery* by a remote manipulator arm and released into orbit.**

EXPLORING THE EARTH FROM SPACE

Observation satellites gather information about the earth's surface that is used in many different ways. Specialist scanners housed in Landsat satellites, for example, produce images that distinguish between different types of open water, rocks, and vegetation. Geologists are able to use Landsat data to locate underground mineral deposits. Environmentalists can monitor significant changes to the earth's surface, such as the destruction of rain forests, the melting of polar ice, and erosion along rivers and coasts. Cartographers use satellite images to draw accurate maps.

EXPLORING THE UNIVERSE

Since the 1970s NASA has launched a series of powerful earth-orbiting space telescopes. Such telescopes, with a view of the universe that is unobstructed by the earth's atmosphere, offer a clearer picture of space than that of earthbound optical telescopes. The most sophisticated and powerful is the Hubble Space Telescope (HST), placed into orbit about 370 miles (600 km) above the earth by the crew of the space shuttle *Discovery* in 1990.

FINDING THE WAY

The Global Positioning System (GPS) is a network of twenty-four satellites that provide navigational information. The satellites broadcast signals that can be picked up on earth by a small GPS receiver. By analyzing the exact source of any four signals and the time it has taken them to travel from the satellite, the receiver is able to pinpoint its precise location

Satellite Orbits

Low earth-orbiting satellites travel at altitudes as low as three hundred miles (480 km) and generally follow a polar orbit (a path that takes them over both Poles). Networks of satellites are arranged in such a way that at least one satellite is on a line of sight with any point on the earth at any given moment. They are close enough to the earth to take detailed photographs of its surface.

Geostationary satellites orbit at an altitude of 22,300 miles (35,890 km). At this height their orbital velocity matches the speed of the earth's rotation, and they remain over the same part of the earth. Three geostationary satellites, positioned 120 angular degrees apart, can provide coverage of the entire world. Geostationary satellites are used for communications and for monitoring the weather.

Some satellites orbit the earth on an elliptical (oval) path. Such satellites pass above the earth's surface more quickly at their lowest altitude, or perigee, and more slowly at their highest altitude, or apogee. They are used for communications by amateur radio operators and by some commercial and government services. In order to pick up transmissions, an antenna has to be adjusted to follow the satellite's path across the sky.

on the planet. GPS is of great use to navigators at sea and in the air and to civil engineers planning the location of new structures.

FORECASTING THE WEATHER

Several satellites, including *TIROS* (Television Infra-Red Observation Satellite), launched in 1960, and *Nimbus,* launched in 1964, provide meteorological data, such as wind speed and direction, cloud formations, and temperature changes in the atmosphere. Meteorologists use such data to predict future weather. Weather forecasts compiled using satellite information are especially useful to explorers when planning their route. A forecast of bad weather may persuade a mountaineer or a polar explorer to remain at base camp until the danger has passed.

SEE ALSO
- Astronomy • Communication Devices
- Global Positioning System • NASA
- Remote Sensing • Space Exploration
- Weather Forecasting

Left **Skylab,** the first U.S. space station, is shown orbiting the earth in 1973.

SCANDINAVIA

THE REGION OF SCANDINAVIA comprises present-day Norway, Sweden, Denmark, and (by some reckonings) Finland, as well as Iceland and the Faeroe Islands. During the early Middle Ages, Scandinavia was the homeland of the Vikings, who made their presence felt throughout Europe and beyond. A number of remarkable journeys to the North and South Poles around the start of the twentieth century inaugurated a second great era of Scandinavian exploration.

Below **Viking longships were exceptionally sturdy and ranged in length from forty-five to seventy-five feet (14–23 m).**

RAIDERS AND TRADERS

Supreme shipbuilders and navigators, the Vikings, or Norsemen, flourished from around 790 to 1100. Some groups (mainly from Sweden) sailed into the Baltic Sea and from there advanced into the interior of Europe and even as far as western Asia. Other groups, principally Danes, sailed southwest to Britain and Ireland, where they eventually seized control of significant territories. Norsemen from Denmark and Norway colonized northern France, where they became known as the Normans. Normans also established a strong presence in the Mediterranean, particularly in southern Italy.

EXPLORATION OF THE NORTH ATLANTIC

From the late eighth century, Norsemen sailed westward into the North Atlantic. The first settlements were built on the Scottish island groups of Orkney, Shetland, and the Hebrides. From these settlements the Norsemen explored farther and reached the Faeroe Islands at the beginning of the ninth

c. 790
Viking raids in western Europe begin.

c. 1000
Leif Eriksson lands in North America.

1354
Paul Knutson is commissioned by the Norwegian king to sail to Greenland.

MARCH 29, 1638
The Swedish ship *Kalmar Nyckel* lands at Delaware in North America.

1728
Vitus Bering proves that Alaska and Siberia are separated by water.

1753–1778
Carolus Linnaeus publishes *Species Plantarum*.

1879
Adolf Nordenskiöld completes the Northeast Passage.

1893–1896
Fridtjof Nansen attempts to reach the North Pole in the *Fram*.

Right **The Kensington Stone, a two-hundred-pound (90 kg) slab of gray sandstone housed in a museum in Alexandria, Minnesota, is either evidence of a fourteenth-century Viking incursion into North America or an entertaining hoax.**

The Kensington Stone

*I*n 1898 a Swedish American named Olaf Oleson, who lived near Kensington, Minnesota, claimed to have uncovered a large, flat, gray stone carved with an inscription dated 1362 and written in Scandinavian runes. Some historians believe the stone supports the theory that a Norwegian expedition reached North America in the fourteenth century. A voyage led by Paul Knutson is known to have been sent to Greenland in 1354. According to the theory, after being blown off course to America, Knutson's party sailed inland up the Nelson River and settled among the Mandans, a Native American people. Several explorers, including Pierre Gaultier de la Vérendrye in 1738 and Meriwether Lewis and William Clark in 1804, reported the Mandans as being Scandinavian in their appearance and habits.

Other historians dismiss this theory and regard the Kensington Stone as a hoax. Some language experts claim that the inauthentic runic language gives the stone away as a clever forgery.

1906
Roald Amundsen completes the Northwest Passage.

1911
Amundsen reaches the South Pole.

1995
Borge Ousland becomes the first person to ski solo to both the North and the South Poles.

2001
Borge Ousland becomes the first explorer to cross Antarctica and the Arctic Ocean.

century, Iceland around 860, and Greenland about 900. Around 1000 they landed in North America.

After the eleventh century the age of Viking expansion came to an end. Throughout Europe, Viking settlers integrated themselves into local populations and began to lose their distinctively Scandinavian character.

Despite one possible incursion into America around 1360 and a Swedish settlement of Delaware in 1638, there seem to have been few notable Scandinavian voyages of exploration from the thirteenth century until the eighteenth.

Linnaeus and His Students

The Swedish botanist Carolus Linnaeus (1707–1778) is best known for the first systematic classification of plants, animals, and minerals. He compiled and updated his botanical works with data from all over the world—yet rarely traveled beyond Scandinavia. Instead, from 1742 Linnaeus sent his students at Uppsala University around the world. Several of them became respected scholars in their own right. Daniel Solander (1733–1782) introduced Linnaean botany to England before joining James Cook's *Endeavour* voyage to the South Pacific (1768–1771). Carl Peter Thunberg (1743–1828) traveled in Japan and, for his study of the plants of the Cape Colony, became known as the father of South African botany.

The Northeast Passage

From the fifteenth century, the desire to find navigable sea routes from Europe to Asia drove many explorers to search for a passage across northern Russia—a northeast passage, as it was known. The possibility that such a route might be found was established by the Dane Vitus Bering (1681–1741). In 1728 Bering

Right **An eighteenth-century portrait of Carolus Linnaeus, one of the most important figures in Scandinavian science and the father of systematic botany.**

discovered that no land bridge connected Siberia and North America (the strait that separates the two landmasses now bears his name). The Northeast Passage was first completed in 1879 by the Norwegian explorer Nils Adolf Erik Nordenskiöld.

THE ARCTIC

Nordenskiöld also led several important Arctic expeditions to Spitsbergen and Greenland. Other notable Scandinavian explorers of the Arctic include the Swede Salomon August Andrée, who explored the Arctic by balloon during an attempt to reach the North Pole in 1897. Otto Neumann Sverdrup, a Norwegian, explored the southern and western coasts of Ellesmere Island, Canada, between 1898 and 1902. The Danes Knud Rasmussen and Peter Freuchen explored and charted northern Greenland and established an exploring station at Thule in 1910.

THE POLES

In 1893 the Norwegian Fridtjof Nansen (who had already made the first crossing of Greenland) allowed a reinforced boat, the *Fram,* to become trapped in the ice so that it would drift toward the North Pole. When it became clear that the ice would not carry the *Fram* all the way, Nansen and a crewmate, Hjalmar Johansen, set off on an epic trek. Although they did not reach the Pole, they reached a more northerly latitude than any explorer had done before.

In 1906 Nansen's protegé, Roald Amundsen (1872–1928), became the first explorer to complete the Northwest Passage, through the Canadian Arctic. In 1910 Amundsen sailed to the Antarctic in Nansen's *Fram,* and on December 14, 1911, he became the first explorer to reach the South Pole.

SEE ALSO

- Amundsen, Roald • Bering, Vitus Jonassen
- Erik the Red • Gudrid • Heyerdahl, Thor
- Leif Eriksson • Nansen, Fridtjof • Natural Sciences
- Nordenskiöld, Nils Adolf Erik • Polar Exploration

Above **Dr. Knud Rasmussen (1879–1933), of Danish and Inuit descent, made a comprehensive study of the native peoples of the vast North American Arctic, especially those of northern Greenland. He described his 1921–1924 expedition, the longest dogsled journey to that time, in** *Across Arctic America* **(1927).**

SCOTT, ROBERT FALCON

THE BRITISH NAVAL OFFICER Robert Falcon Scott (1868–1912), often referred to simply as Scott of the Antarctic, is one of the great heroes of polar exploration. Although he failed narrowly in his attempt to become the first person to reach the South Pole, Scott's two Antarctic expeditions resulted in a much greater understanding of the geography of the continent. Scott's achievements, however, are overshadowed for many by the tragic way in which he and his companions met their death.

Below **Captain Robert Scott, photographed in full ceremonial Royal Navy uniform.**

THE DISCOVERY VOYAGE

In 1901, at the invitation of the Royal Society and the Royal Geographical Society, Robert Falcon Scott led the British National Antarctic Expedition. The simple aim of this expedition was to discover more about Antarctica. Among the crew of Scott's ship, HMS *Discovery*, were Ernest Shackleton and Edward Wilson, both of whom would later achieve fame as polar explorers in their own right.

From its base at the edge of the Ross Ice Shelf, the expedition made several exploratory journeys inland, including an attempt to reach the South Pole. On December 28, 1902, Scott, Wilson, and Shackleton passed 82° south latitude—a distance farther south than any human had ever traveled. Exhausted and sick, they were forced to turn back and only narrowly managed to make it back to their base camp. When he returned to England in 1904, Scott received a hero's welcome.

RACE TO THE SOUTH POLE

Scott's second attempt to reach the South Pole began in June 1910. While sailing down to the Antarctic, Scott learned that the Norwegian explorer Roald Amundsen had also decided to try to reach the Pole. Scott's expedition had turned into a race.

In November 1911 Scott set off across the polar ice with four other men: Edward Wilson, Henry Bowers, Lawrence Oates, and Edgar Evans. The team had intended to use ponies and motorized tractors to help pull the heavy sleds to the foot of the Beardmore glacier, but when those methods proved inadequate, the men had no choice but to haul the loads much of the way themselves. After a punishing eighty-one-day trek, Scott and his men, all of them exhausted and suffering from scurvy, arrived at the South Pole on January 18, 1912—only to find one of Amundsen's abandoned tents. The race was over, and the Norwegian had won.

Transport Trouble

Scott is often criticized for his unwillingness to make use of proven polar transport techniques, such as dogs and skis. American and Norwegian explorers had already demonstrated that such methods—used by the Inuit and other native peoples of the Arctic—were the best way of proceeding across the snow and ice.

Scott did use dogs and skis on his first Antarctic expedition but without a great deal of success. Therefore, on his second expedition he chose to use Manchurian ponies (native to northeastern China). These ponies required substantial supplies of hay for food (notably absent in the vegetation-free Antarctic) and were unable to cope with the extreme conditions. All Scott's ponies perished. Scott also brought three motorized tractors. One sank beneath broken ice the instant it was unloaded, and the other two soon broke down in the extreme cold.

Above **This photograph, taken on February 21, 1911, shows three of Scott's team manhauling their sled across the ice.**

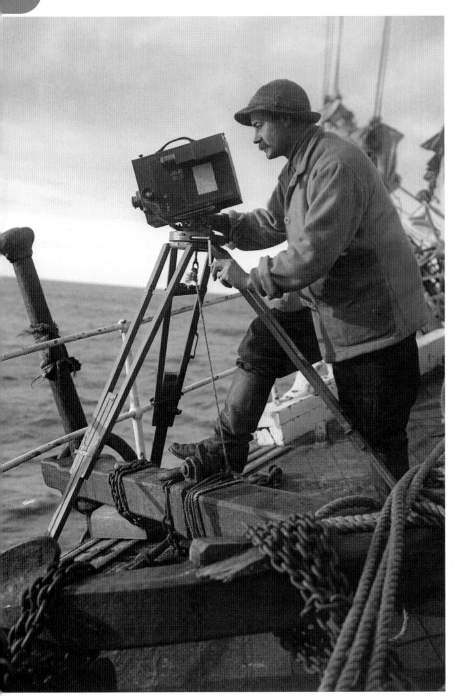

TRAGEDY AWAITS

Scott's realization that, despite his efforts, he had been beaten to the Pole was a devastating blow. He and his men now faced an arduous return journey of over eight hundred miles (1,287 km) in unusually bad weather. They also had to cope with a serious shortage of supplies, which resulted in part from Scott's decision to take a five-man team to the Pole instead of the four-man team that had originally been planned.

On February 7 Edgar Evans fell into a crevasse, and ten days later he died. Lawrence Oates, whose feet were badly frostbitten, became increasingly concerned that he was slowing his companions down. On March 17, with his feet turning gangrenous, he chose to walk out of his tent into a blizzard and certain death. He took his leave with the unforgettable words, "I'm just going outside and may be some time."

THE END OF THE EXPEDITION

On March 21 Scott, Bowers, and Wilson made their final camp. Although they were only eleven miles (18 km) from a fuel and food depot, a ferocious blizzard made any further progress impossible. On or around March 29, with the storm still howling outside, Scott wrote a series of letters that would ensure him lasting fame. Then he and his two companions retired to their sleeping bags and waited to die.

It was not until November 1912 that a search party could be sent out to look for

Above **Scott's expedition was filmed and photographed by Herbert Ponting, pictured here taking footage of whales as they pass close to the *Terra Nova*.**

JUNE 6, 1868
Robert Falcon Scott is born in Devonport, England.

1883
Joins the Royal Navy as a junior officer.

1901–1904
As leader of the British National Antarctic Expedition, reaches a latitude of 82°17' south, five hundred miles (800 km) from the South Pole.

SEPTEMBER 1904
Returns to Britain and is greeted as a hero.

JUNE 1910
Sets off on his second polar expedition.

NOVEMBER 1, 1911
Begins the trek from the coast to the South Pole.

JANUARY 18, 1912
Reaches the South Pole with four others.

MARCH 29, 1912
Dies shortly after making final entry in his diary.

Scott and his men. The tent was found on November 12. The bodies inside had been perfectly preserved by the polar cold. Having buried Scott and his companions, the search party returned to England with Scott's journals and letters. They also took back rock samples collected by Scott and his men on their trek back to base. Later analysis of these rocks proved that Antarctica had once been part of a much larger, forested continent with a temperate climate.

Scott and his team were immortalized in books and on film to the extent that the fame of their failure far outstripped that of Amundsen's success. Scott has been remembered chiefly for the heroic virtues he showed in the face of overwhelming odds and for the honorable way in which he went to his death and less for the substantial new knowledge he provided about the mysterious and awesome continent of Antarctica.

Before his death, Scott wrote a "Message to the Public," which included the following lines:

Had we lived, I should have had a tale to tell of the hardihood, endurance, and courage of my companions which would have stirred the heart of every Englishman. These rough notes and our dead bodies must tell the tale. . . .

Robert F. Scott, March 25, 1912

SEE ALSO
- Amundsen, Roald • Great Britain
- Land Transport • Polar Exploration
- Shackleton, Ernest Henry • Southern Continent

Below **Captain Oates's supreme act of self-sacrifice added further to the heroic status accorded to Scott and his team.**

SETI (Search for Extraterrestrial Intelligence)

ESTABLISHED IN 1984 and based in the United States, SETI (Search for Extraterrestrial Intelligence) is the world's most extensive ongoing project in the search for intelligent life forms elsewhere in the universe. The SETI institute, whose mission is "to explore, understand and explain the origin, nature and prevalence of life in the universe," receives and analyzes radio signals from space in the hope of finding a signal sent out by a technologically advanced extraterrestrial civilization.

Below **Frank Drake, one of the most significant figures in the search for extraterrestrial intelligence, continues to serve as chairman emeritus of SETI.**

The History of SETI

Although fictional accounts of life on other planets were written as early as the eighteenth century, the first systematic search for intelligent life elsewhere in the universe did not begin until 1960. In that year, Frank Drake, a young astronomer in West Virginia, used a radio telescope to carry out the first search for radio waves of extraterrestrial origin.

Drake spent 150 hours on his search, which he called Project Ozma. Though his project failed to find any proof of its existence, Drake did generate a great deal of worldwide interest in the search for extraterrestrial intelligence. According to Drake's Green Bank equation, the nearest advanced extraterrestrial civilization would live only a few hundred light years from earth. By the end of the 1970s, both the Soviet Union and the United States were engaged in the search.

April 1960
Frank Drake uses a radio telescope to listen for extraterrestrial signals.

1960s
Astronomers in the Soviet Union begin to search for extraterrestrial intelligence.

1970s
U.S. radio astronomers join the search.

1980
The Planetary Society is founded by Carl Sagan and others to encourage exploration of the solar system and the search for extraterrestrial intelligence.

November 20, 1984
The SETI Institute is formed.

1992
NASA inaugurates its two largest SETI projects, using the Arecibo radio telescope in Puerto Rico and the Deep Space Communications Center in the Mojave Desert of California.

RADIO WAVES AND INTERFERENCE

SETI astronomers, theorizing that a technological civilization is likely to use radio waves to communicate, generally restrict their search to the radio portion of the electromagnetic spectrum. Yet the universe is filled with radio signals produced by nonintelligent objects, such as stars. It is thought that these signals could interfere with any weaker radio signals deliberately transmitted from faraway planets. However, there is one area of the radio spectrum that contains little interference. SETI astronomers think that intelligent extraterrestrials will also have identified this area of the spectrum as the best means of communicating across the universe and will transmit any messages on those radio frequencies.

This statement from the SETI Institute, founded in 1984, shows its confidence that extraterrestrial life will be found:

SETI, the Search for Extraterrestrial Intelligence, is an exploratory science that seeks evidence of life in the universe by looking for some signature of its technology. Our current understanding of life's origin on Earth suggests that given a suitable environment and sufficient time, life will develop on other planets. Whether evolution will give rise to intelligent, technological civilizations is open to speculation. However, such a civilization could be detected across interstellar distances, and may actually offer our best opportunity for discovering extraterrestrial life in the near future.

1993
NASA cancels its SETI funding.

1994
SETI Institute becomes privately funded.

FEBRUARY 1995
Project Phoenix carries on the work of the NASA SETI project.

1999
The SETI@home project begins.

Above **The Arecibo radio telescope, the largest single-dish telescope in the world, measures one thousand feet (305 m) across and is situated in a natural crater in the mountains of Puerto Rico. SETI astronomers source much of their data from Arecibo.**

Above **An astronomer works in the observing room of the Arecibo radio telescope.**

SETI PROJECTS

Project Phoenix was established in 1995 to search the areas surrounding one thousand sunlike stars. These stars, all within two hundred light years of the earth, are thought to be the most likely to have planetary systems capable of supporting life.

Optical SETI experiments search the visible phenomena of the universe for powerful light pulses that might have been transmitted by advanced extraterrestrial civilizations.

THE FUTURE OF SETI RESEARCH

Although no proof of extraterrestrial life has yet been found, SETI astronomers remain hopeful of success. Future projects will look at different areas of the radio spectrum. New radio telescopes, such as the Allen Telescope Array, will be used solely for SETI research

SEE ALSO

• Astronomical Instruments • Astronomy
• Otherworlds

SETI INSTRUMENTS

Among the data-gathering instruments used by SETI radio astronomers are the Arecibo telescope in Puerto Rico, the largest single-dish telescope in the world, and the Parkes telescope in New South Wales, Australia, the largest radio telescope in the Southern Hemisphere.

SHACKLETON, ERNEST HENRY

CHARISMATIC AND DARING, Ernest Shackleton (1874–1922) is one of the legendary British explorers of the twentieth century. Yet in common with his contemporary and fellow polar explorer Robert Falcon Scott, Shackleton is remembered principally for an expedition that failed in its objective. During his attempt to make the first crossing of the Antarctic continent, Shackleton's ship, the *Endurance,* sank and left the expedition members stranded on the ice. Astonishingly, through a combination of inspired leadership, ingenuity, and sheer determination, Shackleton saved the life of every member of his crew.

Below **This early-twentieth-century photograph captures Shackleton's steely determination.**

FIRST TRIPS TO THE ANTARCTIC

Ernest Henry Shackleton came from a wealthy Irish family and was educated in England. At the age of sixteen, he left boarding school and went to sea with the British merchant marine. He joined his first expedition to the Antarctic in 1901, when he served as a junior officer aboard HMS *Discovery* under the command of Captain Robert Falcon Scott. On this expedition he was a member of Scott's sledding team, which explored the interior of the continent and traveled beyond 82° south latitude, farther south than anyone had ventured before. During the journey, disagreements between Shackleton and Scott ensured that the two men would never work together again. Shackleton became seriously ill with scurvy and was sent home early to recover.

In 1907 Shackleton returned to the Antarctic, this time as leader of his own expedition. In an attempt to be the first person to reach the South Pole, Shackleton set out with a sled party from his ship, *Nimrod*. He got to within ninety-seven miles (156 km) of the South Pole but was eventually driven back by bad weather, exhaustion, and hunger. Nevertheless, Shackleton's achievement made him a national hero, and in 1909 he received a knighthood.

Harry "Chips" McNeish DIED 1930

The ship's carpenter—and owner of the ship's cat, Mrs. Chippy—was the unsung hero of the *Endurance*. His extraordinary improvisational skill with wood ensured that the boats that sailed to Elephant Island and South Georgia were seaworthy. He was even prepared to try to build a smaller ship from the wreck of the *Endurance*. McNeish was one of the six who made the voyage to South Georgia in an open boat.

In his lifetime, McNeish's contribution to the survival of the *Endurance* crew was scarcely recognized. Bad-tempered and disliked by many of his colleagues, he was one of only four members of the crew whom Shackleton did not recommend for a medal on their return to England. McNeish, for his part, never forgave Shackleton for shooting his cat when the *Endurance* had to be abandoned. (All the ship's animals were shot because food was scarce.)

THE *ENDURANCE* EXPEDITION

In 1911 the race to reach the South Pole was finally won by the Norwegian explorer Roald Amundsen. Shackleton turned his attention to a new adventure. In 1914 he returned to the Antarctic for a third time, with the grandly named Imperial Trans-Antarctic Expedition. His aim was to make the first crossing of the entire continent.

Left The expedition's photographer, Frank Hurley, took this shot of Shackleton's *Endurance* trapped in the polar ice.

FEBRUARY 17, 1874
Ernest Henry Shackleton is born in Kilkea, County Kildare, Ireland.

1890
Joins the merchant marine.

1901–1903
Takes part in Scott's *Discovery* expedition to the Antarctic.

1907–1909
During his second Antarctic voyage, in the *Nimrod*, gets to within ninety-seven miles (156 km) of the South Pole.

1909
Receives a knighthood for his services to exploration.

AUGUST 1914
The Imperial Trans-Antarctic Expedition sets off from England.

JANUARY 1915
Endurance becomes trapped in the ice.

NOVEMBER 1915
Endurance sinks; its crew camps on the drifting pack ice.

APRIL 1916
The crew takes to the sea in lifeboats and reaches Elephant Island.

May 20, 1916: After a 36-hour march, Shackleton walks into Stromness whaling station.

May 10, 1916: Shackleton reaches South Georgia.

May 19, 1916: Shackleton sets off for Stromness.

August 30, 1916: Shackleton returns to Elephant Island and rescues his men.

April 15, 1916: Shackleton's party reaches Elephant Island in lifeboats.

April 24, 1916: Shackleton leaves for South Georgia in the *James Caird*.

January 18, 1915: *Endurance* is beset.

November 21, 1915: *Endurance* sinks.

SOUTH ATLANTIC OCEAN

INDIAN OCEAN

Antarctic Circle

South Georgia

South Sandwich Islands

Elephant Island

Princess Martha Coast

Queen Maud Land

Enderby Land

Luitpold Coast

Bellingshausen Sea

Antarctic Peninsula

Ellsworth Land

Marie Byrd Land

Amundsen Sea

South Polar Plateau

South Pole

December 1908: Shackleton climbs the 7,200-foot (2,200 m) Beardmore Glacier to reach the South Polar Plateau.

January 9, 1909: Shackleton reaches 88°07' S.

Beardmore Glacier

Ross Ice Shelf

December 30, 1902: Scott and Shackleton reach 82°17' S.

Princess Elizabeth Land

Wilhelm II Land

Queen Mary Land

Wilkes Land

George V Land

Ross Sea

Cape Adare

→ Route of Scott's sledding team (1902)

→ Route of Shackleton's sledding team (1908–1909)

→ Route of Shackleton and the *Endurance* crew (1914–1916)

→ Shackleton's rescue mission

0   1,000 miles

0   1,500 km

Left **Shackleton's eight-hundred-mile (1,300 km) open-boat journey from Elephant Island to South Georgia, which resulted in the rescue of his crew, ranks as one of the most stirring episodes in the history of exploration.**

In January 1915 Shackleton's ship, *Endurance*, became trapped in the pack ice surrounding Antarctica. After ten months, crushed by the pressure of the ice, the *Endurance* sank. Shackleton was stranded one thousand miles (1,600 km) from the nearest human activity with no hope of rescue.

The twenty-eight members of the expedition party camped on the ice and drifted north for the next five months. Eventually, they reached the edge of the pack ice and were able to launch three boats that had been salvaged from the *Endurance*. After a seven-day journey, they reached uninhabited Elephant Island, in the South Shetlands.

Still without hope of rescue, Shackleton and five of his men set off from this barren rock in the twenty-two-foot (6.7 m) *James Caird*. Shackleton's aim was to reach South Georgia, an island eight hundred miles (1,300 km) to the east. Sailing across some of the roughest seas in the world, Shackleton completed the trip in sixteen days, a remarkable feat of navigation.

APRIL–MAY 1916
Shackleton and five others sail from Elephant Island to South Georgia; Shackleton and two crew members cross the island to reach help.

AUGUST 1916
Shackleton leads the party that rescues the remaining members of the *Endurance* crew from Elephant Island.

1921
Sails to the Antarctic on his final expedition.

1922
Dies of a heart attack at sea, off South Georgia.

The *James Caird* was forced to land on the southern side of South Georgia. The whaling station at Stromness, which offered the men their only chance of rescue, was on the northern side. In a final bid to reach help, Shackleton and two shipmates, Frank Worsley and Thomas Crean, made a daring crossing of the snow-capped mountains of the island.

The Long Wait

*T*wenty-two men were left on Elephant Island when Shackleton sailed for help. Restricted to a narrow, rocky shore, they overturned the remaining boats and used them as shelters. They lived off penguins, sea birds, and the occasional seal. Using penguin and seal fat for fuel, the men kept a fire burning and melted ice for drinking water. As the days grew shorter, hope of rescue before the Antarctic winter began to fade. Shackleton finally reached them on August 30, 1916.

Below **From the coast of Elephant Island, Shackleton's men wave farewell to the *James Caird*, a tiny rowing boat that carries their only hope of rescue.**

It would be nearly forty years before a crossing of the island was attempted again—and then only by skilled mountaineers.

Shackleton, Worsley, and Crean arrived at the whaling station on May 20, 1916. Even then, it took four attempts and three more months for Shackleton to return to Elephant Island and rescue his men. "Not a man lost and we have been through Hell," he wrote proudly to his wife. The story of Shackleton and the *Endurance* is one of the most extraordinary survival stories of all time.

FINAL JOURNEY

Shackleton set out for the Antarctic again in 1921, with many of the men who had been with him on the *Endurance*. In January 1922, just as his ship reached South Georgia, he suffered a fatal heart attack and was buried on the island.

SEE ALSO

• Polar Exploration • Scott, Robert Falcon

GLOSSARY

amidships Toward the part of a ship midway between the bow (at the front) and the stern (at the rear).

Aragon With Castile, one of the two powerful Spanish kingdoms of the late Middle Ages (Aragon and Castile were united in 1479).

cartography The science and art of mapmaking.

conquistador The Spanish word for "conqueror"; specifically, any of the soldiers, explorers, or settlers who, in the wake of Columbus's discovery of the Americas, helped to establish the Spanish presence in Central and South America during the sixteenth century.

electromagnetic spectrum The range of all known wave energy in the universe, including visible light, invisible light (such as infrared and ultraviolet), and radio waves.

extraterrestrial Referring to something whose origin is somewhere other than Earth.

frequency A mathematical property (the number of oscillations per second) that distinguishes one form of wave energy from another.

frostbite A medical condition in which skin and underlying tissues freeze. If blood circulation is not restored to the affected area, frostbite degenerates into gangrene.

gangrene A condition, caused by loss of blood supply to an area of the body, that causes the flesh to rot.

hold The interior area of a ship where cargo and the crew's food stores are generally carried.

Louisiana Territory The land west of the Mississippi River, encompassing the drainage basins of the Missouri and Arkansas Rivers, purchased by President Thomas Jefferson from France in 1803.

magnetosphere A layer that surrounds a celestial object (such as Earth), that is dominated by the object's magnetic field, and within which highly charged particles are trapped.

Mandan A member of a Native American people related to the Sioux who lived along the Missouri River between the Heart and Little Missouri Rivers.

merchant marine A nation's commercial ships, as opposed to those used for military purposes. The merchant marine is in some nations privately owned and in others controlled by the government.

meteorology The study of the weather, especially as a means of forecasting future weather conditions.

micrometeorite A tiny piece of space debris.

Moor A member of a Muslim people of mixed North African, Berber, and Spanish descent who ruled a progressively smaller area of Spain from the tenth century through the fifteenth.

multispectral scanner A remote-sensing device that contains several sensors, each equipped to detect and receive signals from a particular band of the electromagnetic spectrum.

radiate To emit energy in the form of particles or rays.

scurvy A serious disease caused by lack of vitamin C; its symptoms include bleeding and sponginess in the gums.

Shoshone A member of a Native American people who lived by hunting and gathering in the Great Basin region and the northern Rocky Mountains.

solar system A group of celestial bodies that are held by the magnetic attraction of the star they orbit.

synthesis The combination of several concepts or component parts into a single entity.

Taino A member of a Caribbean people native to the Greater Antilles (the islands of Hispaniola, Puerto Rico, Cuba, and Jamaica).

topography The physical features of an area, such as mountains, valleys, and streams; also, the study and mapping of such features.

trading post In North America, a settlement where European traders and Native American hunters exchanged goods for furs.

INDEX

Page numbers in **boldface** type refer to main articles. Page numbers in *italic* type refer to illustrations.

Africa 573, 574
Albuquerque, Afonso de 574, 576
America, Russians in 613
American West 577–580
Amundsen, Roald 627, 628–629, 636
Antarctic exploration 581, 602, 613, 628–631, 635–638
Arctic exploration 583, 614, 627
artists, official 603–604
Asia, central 585–588
aviators, long-distance 615

Bellingshausen, Fabian Gottlieb von 613, 614
Bering, Vitus 626–627
British National Antarctic Expedition 628–631

Cape of Good Hope 573, 575
cartography 591, 639
Charbonneau, Toussaint 616–618
China 564–568, 585, 586, 608–611
Chinese society 568
classical learning 591
Colorado River 577–580
conquistador 569, 572, 639
Copernicus, Nicolaus 591

Dalai Lama 588
Dark Ages 591
digital camcorder 604
Drake, Francis 598
Drake, Frank 632
drinking supplies 581–582

East Indies 573, 576
El Dorado 598, 600
electromagnetic spectrum 605, 605–606, 633, 639
Elizabeth I 598, 600
Endurance 635, 636–637
extraterrestrial 632, 639

Florida 569, 570
food supplies 582–583
Forbidden City see Lhasa
fountain of youth 570, 571
freshwater 597
frostbite 630, 639

Gagarin, Yury 615
gangrene 630, 639
geocentric universe 590
geography, Ptolemaic 591–593
Global Positioning System (GPS) 622–623
Grand Canyon 577–580
Grenville, Richard 598, 599
Gulf Stream 569, 571, 572

Heliocentric universe 591
Henry the Navigator 573–574

India, Portuguese exploration of route to 573, 575

Jesuits 608–609

Kensington Stone 625
Kublai Khan 564, 566–568

Land, management of, in American West 580
latitude 592
Lewis and Clark expedition 616–618
Lhasa 588
Lind, James 584
Linnaeus, Carolus 626
Louisiana Territory 616, 639
Loyola, Ignatius 609

Macao 576, 608–610
McNeish, Harry "Chips" 636
magnetosphere 620, 639
Mandan 625, 639
map projection, Ptolemy's 592
memory skills 608, 610
Mendaña de Neira, Alvaro 594–595
merchant marine 635, 639
meteorology 633, 639
Mongol Empire 564, 566–568
Mongolia 585–588

Moors 569, 639
multispectral scanner 606, 639

North Atlantic, Viking exploration of 624–625
Northeast Passage 626–627
nutrition 584

Oates, Lawrence 630, 631
Ortelius, Abraham 610, 611
Ousland, Borge 627
ozone layer 607

Pacific Ocean 596–597
polar exploration 614, 624, 627, 628–631
transport trouble in 629
Polo, Marco **564–568,** 586
Il Milione 564, 567, 568, 603
Ponce de León, Juan **569–572**
Portugal **573–576**
exploration of Africa 573–574
exploration of India 575–576
potato 599
Powell, John Wesley **577–580**
provisioning **581–584**
Przhevalsky, Nikolay **585–588**
Przhevalsky's horse 587
Ptolemy **589–593**
Puerto Rico 569, 570

Quirós, Pedro Fernández de **594–597**

Radiation 607, 639
Raleigh, Walter **598–600**
record keeping **601–604**
remote sensing **605–607**
Renaissance 591
Ricci, Matteo **608–611**
Roanoke Island 598–599, 603
Ross, John 583
Russia **612–615**
exploration of Antarctica 613
exploration of the Arctic 614
exploration of Asia 585–588, 612
exploration of space 615

Sacagawea **616–618**
satellite communication 621

satellites **619–623**
the first 620
mapping the earth 606–607
observation from space 622
orbits 623
weather 623
Scandinavia **624–627**
Scott, Robert Falcon **628–631**
scurvy 584, 629, 635, 639
SETI (Search for Extraterrestrial Intelligence) **632–634**
Shackleton, Ernest Henry **635–638**
Shoshone 616, 616–618, 639
Silk Road 565
solar system 590, 619, 639
Southern Continent see Terra Australis
space telescopes 622
Spanish explorers 569–572

Taino 569, 570, 572, 639
Terra Australis 594, 595
Tibet 585, 586, 588
tobacco 599
topography 591, 605, 639
Turkistan 585, 586

U.S. Geological Survey 580

Vikings 624–625
Virginia 598

White, John 603